ALL-IN CULTURE

LEAD YOUR PEOPLE TO BE OF SERVICE

CHRIS SMOJE

R^ethink

First published in Great Britain in 2023
by Rethink Press (www.rethinkpress.com)

© Copyright Chris Smoje

To my mum and my dad.

Mum, thank you for reading to me as a child and instilling in me the importance and pleasure of reading.

Dad, your dream of writing a book has inspired me to write mine. Thank you for including me in your many visits to the State Library of Western Australia as you conducted your research.

Contents

Preface

Service Is More Than A Job

When I reflect on my childhood, there is one memory that marked me apart from other children. It's something that made me who I am.

I am the eldest child in my family, and I am a third generation Australian. All four of my grandparents were born in Yugoslavia (now Croatia) and immigrated to Australia before World War II. My parents raised me with a strong connection to my ancestry, but it was my dad who played a pivotal role.

As an active member of the Croatian community in Perth, he would take me as a child to events and the homes of the early pioneers. These 'old timers' were getting on in life, and my dad would document their reminiscences of immigrating and their early life in Australia. I found it boring to be dragged along and there were other things I'd rather have been doing instead.

I was taught to be respectful to elders. Shaking hands and kissing both cheeks whenever I met someone, right through to having a conversation with them. By the age of four I was having proper conversations, not just small talk, with strangers. When I speak to many of my relatives today, they tell me I could talk with them for hours and take part in grown-up conversations. I learned the art of communication from a young age, which continued into my school years and my first job.

Working on the checkout at a local supermarket as a teenager, I was good at customer service. I received compliments from customers who came through my checkout, as well as commendations from my managers. Even as a fifteen-year-old working only a few hours a week, it was something I loved doing. I continued to work in retail through my high school years and transitioned to the airline industry after university. It was here I noticed an interesting pattern, both for me and my colleagues.

When talking about customer service, we always seemed to refer to the expectations of customers. But what about the expectations we had when providing that service? The staff sometimes also have expectations of their customers. When we start a job, we are trained in the technical elements so that we know our role well – or at least, better than the customer. This illusion gives us the belief that we know everything.

What happens if customers don't behave the way you expect them to? What happens when customers, knowingly or not, don't do the right thing? How should you respond if they are on their mobile phone as you serve them? As I got older and more experienced, I noticed this brought out the worst in people – myself included.

There's a word used to describe this type of judgemental reaction, it's 'moralising'. Many people confuse moralising with demoralising. You demoralise someone by putting them down, so they lose confidence and hope. People think that moralising is opposite, a positive thing, but it isn't. Moralising means to talk to someone with an unfounded air of superiority while commenting on issues of right and wrong – in other words, pushing your morals on to them. Your morals are usually learned from your parents, and we rarely have the same exact morals as one another. As I continued to observe customer service, I realised most of the adversarial situations stemmed from moralising.

Staff in the airline industry would say to customers who missed their flights, 'You should have planned ahead for road-works on the way to the airport', 'You should have left home early to allow enough time', or 'You should have read the terms and conditions of your ticket'. Some customers don't have the capacity to organise themselves or even plan ahead and timekeeping may not even be something they value. Yet, staff would feel compelled to make a moralising comment. Notice how these all start with 'you should have'.

When I became aware of this, I noticed it in other industries and customer service roles too. The fact that people working in customer service were not bringing the best out of themselves was a concern. How could people with supposedly good communication skills and enjoyment of their job become 'moralisers'? Working in customer service doesn't necessarily mean you are providing customer service. Lunchrooms and back of house areas became gossip grounds for criticising customer behaviour and Facebook groups have emerged as an outlet to vent about having to serve. In life, you can choose how you respond to people and situations, and serving customers is no different. Yet people are often reactive toward their customers.

My career soon took me from the delivery of customer service to learning and development roles where I was responsible for delivering customer service training. I quickly found the programs were underdeveloped, out of date or simply non-existent. When I became a leader, I saw this as the opportunity to think about making changes to the training programs, and I also observed how the role of leaders in the business could play a part in creating a culture of service.

I was fortunate to work for an organisation that saw significant transformations in the service culture and when it came time to move on, I knew what I wanted to do in life – to help other organisations create cultures that enabled their people to be of service. I've lived service, taught service and led service, which brings me to write service. My core focus of service and aim in writing this book is to help leaders get their people as far away as possible from the situations where they're about to lose it with their customers. Being of service is one of the best strategies in achieving this.

Introduction

The state of service

There has been a decline of great service over time, but there has also been a slow incline of better service in recent years. A handful of global organisations are doing wonders with their service, and, at the same time, the bar has been raised, in many cases due to technology. This leaves a perpetual gap faced by many organisations. Fundamentally, customer service isn't where it should be and now is the time to do something about it.

I look back at my first few years in the workforce as being integral to who I am today. The major Australian supermarket Coles recently predicted that there would be no checkouts in their stores by 2030.[1] (Note, checkout-less supermarkets such as Amazon Go in the US have been around since 2018.) We will explore the effects of technology and self-service later in this book, but, for now, I think about my children and what job they will have when they are teenagers if checkouts cease to exist. The frontline delivery of customer service at a young age is the perfect place for future leaders to learn what it means to be of service to others.

Why such a focus on service? Aside from it being the essence of everything that occurs within your organisation, it has fast become the only distinguishing factor in business today. When competition is neck to neck on product and technology, it is the service people provide that is the only advantage. Exceptional service is not exclusive; however, as it originates from the unique people within an organisation, it is harder for competitors to copy. This is because they must uncover and nurture this within their own people. According to research by Dimension Data, 81% of organisations cite service experience as a competitive advantage.[2] Many businesses claim their point of difference is exceptional service, but that's often nothing more than clever marketing and lip service. This is an opportunity to make your business stand out from the rest.

Aside from the competition for customers, there is also a war being fought for staff. Just like how the best house won't always be on the property market, the best employee will not be waiting for a job. Nothing is worse than having great staff taken from you by another employer. The stronger your culture of service is, the greater chance you will be able to fight off other prospective employers. It will also make your people happier at work and when they go home to their families, meaning they will be less likely to leave or be lured away. I have witnessed summer seasonal businesses with strong cultures of service where the staff resign from their winter jobs to return to their 'main' job for the summer season.

When a business becomes a force for good, it can positively impact the lives of its customers. Not just the customers being served but the other customers who witness the exceptional service feel good about what they've observed. Business has slowly shifted to focus on profits before people, but when we focus on the service we provide on our frontline, it will ultimately make a positive impact on the bottom line (the metrics for this will be explored later in the book). When an entire organisation can see their service making a difference to customers beyond the functional elements of their work, this is where magic happens.

Leaders need to overmanage service

The Walt Disney Company coined the phrase 'overmanage'.[3] This differs from the traditional negative view of micromanaging. To overmanage means to think about things differently to other organisations by paying attention to the details of service and placing a greater emphasis on service than most organisations would.

Leading a culture that inspires a team to be of service to others is one of the major hurdles as well as one of the top priorities for business leaders according to a survey by Norwegian software company SuperOffice.[4] While leaders recognise they are ultimately responsible for the delivery of service in their organisation, they struggle to be completely responsible because at every moment of the day (or night), someone is doing something to serve, whether it be for an internal customer, external customer or supplier. Service is something that's easy to talk about but hard to lead.

Leaders who see service as something they should be involved in tend to fall into the trap of micromanaging service. This has the reverse effect, making staff members feel restricted, and, in turn, they don't provide the level of service they should. Meanwhile, the leader becomes more stressed and worried about being in control – eventually causing a bottleneck and slowing down any improvement to the service culture.

Everyone in a chief executive role wants to leave their mark and make a positive difference to their organisation. The pressure on a leader is not necessarily just their work-load; it is the pressures they put on to themselves.

We often hear about good leaders 'rising through the ranks', but this is only the case if the leader understood the concept of service from the beginning when they worked on the frontline. If they were prone to 'moralising' their cus-tomers, it's unlikely they will make a positive difference to customer service as a leader. Alternatively, if they understood service but worked with a leader who didn't empower their team, it would be hard for them to see the true value of ser-vice in business.

People and culture – a powerful overlap

I was once having coffee with a colleague of mine and we were talking about having meetings with prospective cli-ents. This person had been a professional speaker far longer than I had and he told me he completely avoids dealing with human resource (HR) departments, as they 'destroy every idea before it gets to the CEO'. This got me thinking about my early exposure to the world of HR.

One of the first conferences I attended was for learning and development professionals held in Sydney. The theme was

'How to remain relevant', based on the notion that training departments and budgets were being cut and the profession was slowly dying.

I soon noticed that because HR departments were protective of their role in the organisation, they wouldn't always work well with other departments.

A relationship exists between leaders and HR, as both roles play a crucial part in building cultures of service, but they don't always do this together. Working with your HR team is like watering a plant. It is essential to keep watering it, but what if the water continues to argue with the soil? The plant will not grow. This is what happens in many organisations between leaders and HR.

There has been a slow shift away from the name 'human resources' to 'people and culture' departments, but the name change is only the beginning. The organisations that make the greatest impact have people in roles such as 'chief customer officer,' someone customer-focused that has a seat at the executive table with open and direct dialogue with the chief executive officer.

The following model shows how the role of a leader integrates with the frontline and people and culture departments. This book addresses the three problems that leaders face:

1. Struggling to be service focused.

2. Struggling to work in partnership with other leaders and HR.

3. Struggling to make a positive difference to the organisational culture.

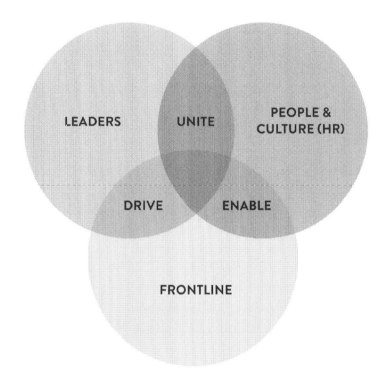

Working Relationships Model

The predictable stages

It is common on any learning journey for people to say they've tried something before and it hasn't worked. Or they look for the easy shortcuts known as 'tips and tricks' and 'hacks'.

This book isn't designed to give you the tricks of the trade, but rather to give you the trade itself. You need this to go 'all in' on your service culture. You might have some people with you on the journey, so the challenge is getting everyone on board. Fortunately, there is a structure, pathway and process you can follow to help empower your people and lead a culture where everyone in your organisation is of service to others.

The chapters are like milestones that help break up the journey, but the thing to remember with any journey is not about what happens at the end, but what happens on the way. The journey starts with you as a leader being exceptional from the beginning. A winning athlete is already warmed up when the race begins, and this book operates in the same way. It's not designed to warm you up. You should be ready to go, and this book will take you through the process.

There are three core sections of the book, shown in the model below. It's about getting you more involved in service culture, defining what success looks like, making it all happen and then knowing how to get out of the way to let your people serve their customers best.

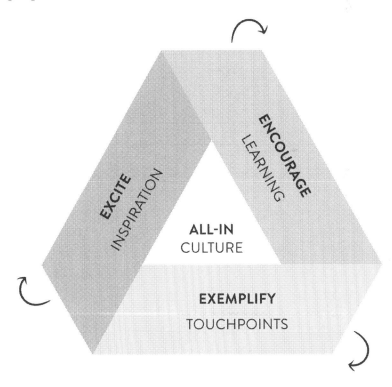

All-In Culture Model

A leader may be able to excite, encourage and be an example to their teams, but they must be able to, among other things, do it in the domain of service culture. Therefore, this book will help you as a leader to learn and develop high standards when leading your people to be of service. As Amazon founder Jeff Bezos said in his 1997 letter to his shareholders, 'There can be whole arenas of endeavor where you may not even know that your standards are low or non-existent, and certainly not world class. It's critical to be open to that likelihood.'[5]

The first part of the book is about creating excitement around serving others. The hardest part is knowing where and how to get started, so this theoretical look at service will inspire you and the rest of your team to get involved. The whole section will prepare you for Part Two.

Once your team are inspired, it will be time to encourage them. Part Two shows you how to encourage your team. Here, we will explore a practical framework for a culture of exceptional service and identify what success looks like. You need to have read Part Two of the book to apply the specific practices discussed in Part Three.

With your team now excited and encouraged, it's up to you to lead by example and prove everything to this point isn't just lip service. The final part of the book will show you how you can make the service culture stick and thrive through your daily activities as a leader, as well as through the key operational touchpoints in your business. As author James Clear said, 'People gravitate toward the standard you set, not the standard you request.'[6]

Notice the arrows on the model showing this as a continuous cycle. This means that you need to be constantly inspiring, encouraging and exemplifying the service culture to the team through your activities. This especially needs to continue when new people join your business.

I find serving others exciting. As an educator, I know encouragement is important, and you must be an example for others to follow. My goal for this book is to create excitement, encourage you and exemplify what it truly means to be of service. Each part addresses the common areas of struggle and offers stories that engage, models to help you put it all together and questions to reflect on, as you become a leader who goes all in and empowers your people to be of service to others.

PART ONE
EXCITE

Over time, the term 'customer service' has become so simplified that its definition is now inaccurate. Often the term brings to mind a call centre operator, receptionist or checkout operator, but this is not what customer service actually is. Some people are also of the opinion that customer service is 'dead'. To change this, we must unlearn what we know about service and relearn it in a contemporary context.

This doesn't mean that simplification is bad, but we must consider whether it is actually useful to simplify things? The problem with service today is that it has been simplified so much that people feel it is no longer useful in the business world. If this is the case, why would we focus on it at all?

There has become a disconnect with the concept of serving others, as well as a reluctance or lack of appetite to improve. Meanwhile service is left behind while business and the marketplace continue to advance.

The most challenging aspect of working with organisations on their service is the perception that service is all 'fluff.' As new and competing fields like technology emerged, organisations have lost sight of it altogether.

Unlearning service

Organisational psychologist and author Adam Grant said, 'Learning is how you evolve. Unlearning is how you keep up as the world evolves.'[7] This is true when it comes to service.

If we are to unlearn service, we must first pick it apart and look at it from a variety of angles to understand what service is. This will help you present it in a new way to inspire your teams to be of service. The four dimensions of 'unlearning service' are shown in the following model.

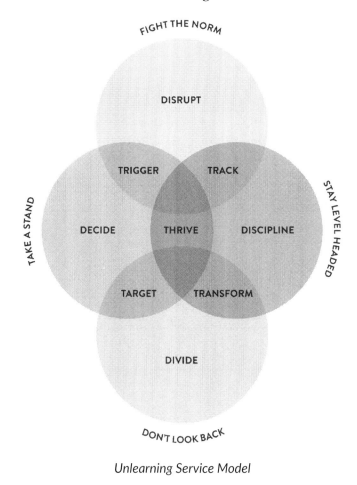

Unlearning Service Model

This first chapter will disrupt some key beliefs about both customers and service separately, which will begin to trigger a change in our service culture. We will then look internally at our people and make some key decisions about the process we are about to embark on, which will help us commit and thrive long term. Next, we will look at the disciplines required so we can stay on track throughout this process. The final section will examine the divide that exists between your current levels of service and the targets we will set to transform your service culture into the future.

The late American writer and business futurist Alvin Toffler once said, 'The illiterate of the 21st century will not be those who cannot read and write, but those who cannot learn, unlearn, and relearn.'[8] Get ready to unlearn customer service as you know it.

QUESTIONS TO CONSIDER

- What core assumptions do you have about customer service?
- Is there anything controversial you think about service?
- Is there any ambiguity in your mind around service?
- How well do you know customer service, really?

1
Disrupt

Old-fashioned customer service for today

I open most of my presentations showing two images of toilet paper side by side. The first, let's call it 'A', shows the toilet paper hanging over the roll, and the second, 'B', shows the toilet paper hanging under the roll. Immediately this creates a reaction among participants, with the majority saying that 'A' is correct, with a few people arguing that it's 'B'.

I then pose the question: what does this have to do with customer service? This is when the audience starts to think a little deeper, and there are five core connections that are commonly made.

First, we have an expectation that when we go to a bathroom there will be toilet paper. Customers also hold expectations that they will receive service wherever they go.

Second, toilet paper is an essential item when we use the bathroom. Customers see service too as something essential to help them navigate around products or services.

Third, if it's missing, or sometimes hung the wrong way, we may complain. Customers often complain when there is an absence of service, or if service isn't delivered in what they believe is a satisfactory way.

Fourth, toilet paper hasn't changed in years; likewise, the essential concept of customer service hasn't changed either.

Finally, the toilet roll can be hung over or under and displayed differently without changing how it's used, just as customer service can be delivered in different ways without there being a right or wrong answer.

If we look at the first three points, the world has developed some perceptions about customers and their expectations, the necessity of service and the way that they complain. These three all relate to the customer. The final two relate to service. Over time, we have developed perceptions of what service is and what we think is the right way to serve a customer.

These five areas are not hidden; they are just ignored. If we continue on this path, some businesses will fall behind while others move forward. Businesses that are leading in customer service have focused on these five areas – it's not too late for you to do the same.

Author Simon Sinek said, 'Our best competitors reveal our weaknesses',[9] which is particularly true in terms of customer service. If you look at most forms of business disruption, it occurs when one person or organisation sees a gap or dated practice that, when improved, will provide a better outcome for the customer.

Looking back to the 1950s, Walt Disney ideated the concept of Disneyland after watching his child play in a dirty amusement park. He could see an opportunity to offer a service that was ultimately better for the customers to experience. When I ask someone to think of examples of old-fashioned service, their face lights up. People smile when they reminisce about their childhood. Even young people are nostalgic about the stories their parents once told them. It's considered to be 'off-trend' when we talk about business in the 'old days', but there's never been a better time to look back fondly on the service we once received and see how we can use this to disrupt the world of service today.

QUESTIONS TO CONSIDER

- How do you stay at the forefront as customers' expectations increase?
- Can you see that the essential element of business is to be of service?
- How can you look at customer complaints differently?
- Has service started to take a different course in your organisation?
- What longstanding customer service clichés can you think of?

The rest of this chapter will explore each of the five perceptions of customers and service further.

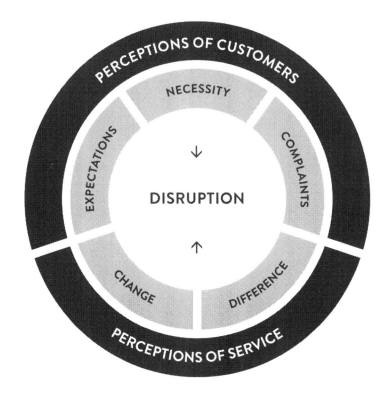

Disruption Model

Expectations come from comparisons

A few summers ago, I went to Croatia with my wife for a six-week holiday. It was a highlight in our lives together. Singapore Airlines, one of the top airlines in the world, renowned for its service to customers, transported us on the main legs of our journey. Here, I want to share with you something that happened on our return home.

We boarded the aircraft at Singapore Changi Airport for the approximately five-hour flight to our home in Perth. We were greeted at the door by the lead flight attendant, given full attention throughout the flight, and a smile and genuine farewell by the same attendant as we left the aircraft.

As Australians returning home, we proceeded through the e-passport gate. We had nothing to declare and picked our car up from the long-term car park at the terminal. Exiting the aircraft to arriving at our front door was done within an hour. It was mid-afternoon and we knew that we would need to head to the shops to pick up some bread and milk. As we arrived at our front door, we noticed a 'sorry we missed you' card for an attempted parcel delivery while we were away, so on our way to the shops, we stopped at the local post office. Keep in mind, the last person we had interacted with was the lead flight attendant at the door of the Singapore Airlines aircraft – and the next person we interacted with was the person behind the desk at the post office.

The lady called 'next in line' when it was our turn. We weren't greeted as she immediately reached for the parcel slip that was in our hands. When she noticed the date was a few weeks old, she remarked that parcels should be picked up within a few days and that she would need to go out back and search for it, which isn't easy. As she came back with the parcel, we were asked to 'sign here' and to show our ID. We were told 'thank you' and, as my wife was still putting her driver's licence back into her purse, the lady called for the next customer. To be honest, the service we received that day was consistent with the service we would normally receive at the post office, but on this occasion it felt different. We noticed it more.

This was because we were directly comparing it to the service we'd received from Singapore Airlines. While a five-star airline and a post office perhaps shouldn't be compared, customers do compare. The person behind the counter wouldn't have had any idea that we had just returned from a holiday (although the date on the delivery slip would have been a good indicator), but what if, for argument's sake, everyone at the post office assumed that all their customers had just got off a flight with an airline like Singapore Airlines?

It used to be acceptable to think that expectations can be framed based on the business or industry. For instance, customers' expectations of a post office would be different to an airline. While this is fair, when a customer receives exceptional service, they will remember it and use it as a reference point when they interact with your organisation, even if the industries are unrelated. Organisations that understand this will always have their sights set on improving service.

It is believed by some that English playwright and poet William Shakespeare once said, 'Expectation is the root of all heartache.' Former US President Theodore Roosevelt echoed this sentiment when he reputedly said, 'Comparison is the thief of joy.' When we were young, we were told to never compare ourselves to others, that everyone is on a unique journey of their own. There's an exception when it comes to service, though. Who are your customers comparing you to? How does your organisation stack up?

When a business uses the phrase 'the best [product] in town' in its marketing, it immediately creates comparison in the customer's mind. While customers will compare whether you like it or not, the challenge lies in the change in their expectations these comparisons lead to.

People can't help but compare. In my workshops I ask participants a simple question: 'Do you like Pepsi?' It always generates some discussion, but every time, the discussion shifts to whether Pepsi is better than Coca-Cola. It's hard to discuss one without the other. The question was whether people liked or disliked the product, not what they'd compare it to.

In Australia, there is a concept known as the 'MKR Effect' which stands for 'My Kitchen Rules Effect'. MKR is a reality cooking show, and it creates customers who become 'culinary armchair experts', putting significant pressure on the wait staff at restaurants. This same effect is seen in hardware stores after reality shows on renovations and home improvements are shown. It's clear that expectations are not just formed by other companies but through TV as well.

Being an armchair expert is often underrated but it can be highly damaging to those who provide service to customers. It's so easy to become an armchair expert; just look at how sports fans easily pick on referees from the grandstands.

As frontline staff are faced with navigating the customer's expectations, the easy way out is to say that their expectations are unrealistic, and that the more you do, the more demanding the customer will become. This is not the case. There is disconnect between the service that staff provide and their own expectations of service. For example, many organisations have timeframes stating they will respond to customers' emails within five to ten business days. Yet, if you ask the same staff concerned how long they believe is reasonable to wait for a reply to an email, they will often say twenty-four to forty-eight hours. This shows that the customer's expectations are not always unrealistic. I'd like to add that the real customer-centric organisations I have come across have a 'sundown' rule where each email is simply acknowledged by the end of the day.

Even if a customer demands something from an organisation, it doesn't necessarily mean they are being difficult, which is another misconception we find when talking to those on the frontline. It's important to acknowledge that customers do expect things quicker today than years ago. With technology giving us immediate access to all manner of things, it's only fair this extends to service.

When I was young, the gameshow *Who Wants to Be a Millionaire?* occupied an hour-long timeslot. The difficult questions would go on for minutes, and sometimes the audience was left hanging until after the commercial break to find out the answer. Watching the show was a family affair. Now the show is in an abridged format with time pressures on each question. This is likely because the audience couldn't resist the urge to Google the answer if it went on too long.

We can use expectations and comparisons to our advantage to lead service, rather than playing catch-up. In other words, your direct competitors are no longer those in your industry; they are anyone who provides better service than you.

Rather than thinking about Singapore Airlines in this instance, it is far more useful to consider a local coffee shop as your main competitor. Assume that all your customers go to the same coffee shop every morning. Every day the barista remembers their order, they ask questions about the family and they know when they've been on holiday. Do your staff remember your customers like a local barista does?

In the hospitality industry, it is fair to assume that customers expect to be able to split their bill when they pay. When a venue doesn't offer this option, they stand out among their competitors – and for the wrong reasons. In 2018, a customer in Perth, Western Australia, not only took a stand and refused to pay if the restaurant didn't split the bill but also published an article on her experience in the local newspaper.[10]

There's no way to escape this. As other businesses offer better service to your customers, they will expect – and demand – the same from you. To stay on the front foot, it's best if you delivered the better service, so they demand the same from others. It's just a case of whether you want to be reactive to service, or proactive.

QUESTIONS TO CONSIDER

- Aside from the coffee shop, do you know other places your customers visit that provide better service than your organisation?
- How do you compare to them?

Customers are deserving of your service

Imagine you are leaving work after having 'one of those days' – a day where everything has gone wrong. You were late, forgot your lunch, the computer system went down, your boss was putting pressure on you and you got a parking fine because you didn't move your car in time. You finally leave the office ready to put the day behind you.

While you're driving, you get a call from someone at home who is cooking dinner. They're short a can of tomatoes and were wondering whether you could swing by the shops and pick one up. You'd prefer not to, but it's on the way so you quickly call into the shops to grab the item.

Your interaction with the person on the checkout doesn't go well. You've had a bad day, but so have they. Their attitude makes your blood boil. It puts you in a worse mood than you already were, and you carry this mood home and rant about it to your family. Has this ever happened to you?

Meanwhile the person at the checkout talks about you to their family. They refer to you as this 'entitled' customer who came in just before close. Would you describe yourself as an entitled customer? Probably not.

When times get tough it's easy to think of customers as being entitled, but it would be helpful to shift the word from entitled to deserving. A deserving customer sounds much better than an entitled customer. An entitled person acts in a demanding way, whereas a deserving person has a deep belief they are worthy of being treated well.

From our outside perspective we can never really know what someone else is going through on a personal level. This is true with all customers. They have jobs and families, and the associated responsibilities like bills to pay. When we recognise this, we realise they deserve the best service possible and that, regardless of the day we're having, we can still make a positive difference to a stressful day for them. We must look at service beyond performing the basic functions of our job to how it makes the customer feel.

The necessity of service, just like the necessity of toilet paper, is not limited to this example. It's not just about customers who have a bad day; service is the essential element of most interactions for many organisations.

With the rise of technology and self-service systems in full swing, the moment of interaction between humans has become critical. When the website doesn't work, when the self-serve scanner doesn't scan, we immediately turn to another human for help.

This is not a debate on whether to adopt technology to replace elements of work originally performed by humans. In fact, given the way many of these tasks were traditionally performed, it's no wonder technology has replaced them. Repetitive tasks that can be automated don't really need a human to do them. People can be critical of organisations adopting self-service technology as a way of cutting jobs, like at the checkout, but if you stopped and asked customers what their biggest pain point in the supermarket was, it would be the checkout.

Think about what happened to you before self-service took off. You'd do your shopping then, when you got to the checkouts, you'd look for the lane with the smallest queue and the fastest operator. You hated the awkwardness of waiting with insincere small talk. Staff will be cut in the long run, but we must ask whether they were effectively serving a human purpose in the first place.

The biggest issue has not been introducing technologies to make the experience for customers better. The issue has been replacing humans, full stop. Technology isn't fool proof, even though it appears to be, so humans are necessary to provide the service when it fails. Australian broadcaster Clive James is believed to have said, 'it's only when they go wrong that machines remind you of how powerful they are.'

One of my favourite customer rants over self-service checkouts goes something like this: 'Unexpected item in the bagging area! How so? You just told me what I scanned – I did my bit, but you haven't done yours. Now you'll alert a human who will come over and think I'm a thief!' If you'd love to hear a comedian's view of self-service, check out Bill Burr's account of having to put his own mayonnaise on a sandwich.[11] It's true the technology may not always be at fault, sometimes the customer may do something that causes it to stop working. However, is it fair to expect customers to know how to do something and work a machine as you would expect your own staff to?

Taking the toilet paper metaphor further, French toilet paper company Le Trèfle produced an advert that centred around a husband and wife at home. Every time the wife did something with paper that could be replaced with technology, her husband would point out that it could be done on a tablet. Until one day he was in the bathroom and the toilet roll was empty. He called his wife, but instead of giving him toilet paper, she slid a tablet under the door with a picture of toilet paper on it. The tag line on screen read 'Paper has a great future'.[12]

Another advert for Norwegian supermarket REMA1000 showed a man in a house where everything was voice activated. Which all worked fine, until he returned to his house in the rain after visiting the dentist with the side effects of anaesthetic numbing his mouth. As a result, the door didn't understand his command, and he was locked out in the rain.[13]

While these two examples show the humorous side of product advertising, they highlight the limitations and shortcomings of technology. When technology fails, it's over to customer service to fix the problem. During the global Covid-19 pandemic, there were predictions that we would never again shake hands again or have face-to-face meetings, but while life has changed, people and your customers still crave connection.

In the Introduction, I framed how important frontline service roles are for young people new to the workplace in helping them to learn essential skills, and I considered my young children and what they will do as their first job. The answer to this will be found in the areas where humans can add value and not be replaced by machines.

In the future, service will be seen as the biggest value add to customers to enhance their experiences, with a huge shift away from transactional roles that perform a function without any emotional value. This trend may well have already started.

In 2019, Australian supermarket retailer Woolworths announced an investment of $10 million into employee train-ing.[14] Primarily, this investment was to give staff a greater understanding of the products on sale so they could help customers decide on the best cuts of meats and products to buy, and how they should be cooked.

Consider how you can ensure with every technology or self-service element present in your business that you can add a personal touch, or have a personal touch available when things go wrong. Your customers will love it. For example, Coca-Cola and Nutella have produced products with people's names on to add the personal element to their customers' experience.

The changing nature of customer complaints

Another myth that we need to disrupt is that 'customers love to complain'. In fact, there is conflicting evidence on both sides of this myth. The 2022 statistics of the Telecommunications Industry Ombudsman in Australia show that the number of complaints is on the rise, with 22,000 customers complaining mostly about customer service and billing.[15] Yet it's possible that customers are complaining less and taking their business elsewhere, or simply staying silent. Research by Esteban Kolsky, CEO of ThinkJar, suggests that only one in twenty-six unhappy customers complains; the rest leave.[16] This silence or loss of customers could give the illusion to many that customers are complaining less.

Whichever way you analyse this, it's important to firstly distinguish how easy it is for customers to complain. If you think about the Telecommunications Industry Ombudsman, it is an avenue for complaints, so it's no wonder why it is getting more of them. As for other industries, it may not be that customers are complaining less; it might be that you're unknowingly making it hard for them to complain.

A few years ago, my wife and I were holidaying in the tourist resort town of Noosa, on the east coast of Australia. We went out to dinner to one of the town's fancier restaurants, which was great and so was the food. The service was fairly good, but there was one thing that could have been done better. We found that there was always something to ask for – first, being ready to order; second, for another drink; third, for the salt and pepper, and so on. We relied more heavily on the wait staff at this restaurant compared to others. We noticed that whenever the wait staff served a table near us, they would turn quickly in the opposite direction (away from the rest of the restaurant) and head straight to the kitchen. This made flagging down a waiter hard, with the only alternative being to call out to them, which we didn't feel comfortable doing.

When we look at complaints or feedback through the eyes of the wait staff, their perception would be that their customers didn't need much from them that night. If we were to complain to the restaurant, it would be a shock to the waiter concerned that we didn't think he was attentive enough. On that occasion we chose not to say anything, but perhaps would have if we were asked about the service when we paid our bill. I wonder why this wasn't built into their payment process.

I recently purchased Mark Manson's *New York Times* Bestseller, *The Subtle Art of Not Giving a F*ck*.[17] When I started to read it, I was confused because the first two pages of the contents were duplicated so I had the first half of the contents twice, but not the second half. It was clearly a glitch in the printing although I did wonder whether Manson was testing his readers to see whether they gave a 'F' about it. As I read the book and considered many of the things that Manson talked about (what to care about and what not to), I wondered whether I should go back to the bookshop and ask for another book. I like referring to the contents page while reading, but while it was frustrating, I let it go.

The more organisations I work with, the more I find there is less upfront feedback from their customers. These same organisations eventually either get complaints fed back to them when customers escalate the situation by emailing someone more senior, bypassing the people on the frontline, or post online via social media. Customers are not complaining early on and in person (or the most direct channel), but there is a deeper problem that has changed the nature of the way customers complain.

Cast your mind back to business from around 2000 to 2010. Email technology was well established and used in businesses, but it was treated as a 'fad' when it came to customer feedback. Meanwhile social media was only emerging and had not been widely embraced as a tool for business. Think about a time when you were a customer during this period, and you approached someone to give them feedback in person. You were often told, 'You'll need to put that in writing', or 'Send us an email to this address detailing your feedback and a manager will get back to you.' Can you imagine for one moment anyone saying that in business today?

For at least a decade, poor service on the frontline slowly educated customers not to complain in person (because nothing ever gets done – true or not), and to go online and complain. Customers are accustomed to this, but now it is hurting businesses more. There are some cultures that love to complain and others that aren't as forthcoming, but that's not the point.

Businesses often fear complaints. They don't empower frontline staff to deal with them in real time. They have amazing marketing teams who can provide better complaint resolution via Twitter than by speaking to a real person. There are algorithms on chatbots that detect the use of certain words to escalate issues quicker than if a real person were dealing with the complaint.

Better service online or via email means the full capabilities of your frontline teams are being wasted. Complaints have transitioned to being not only about the problem itself, but more about how the problem is handled when the customer complains. It's great to have different avenues for complaints, but one of them must be the frontline. With many customers now self-sufficient, it is common in some organisations to only speak to a real person when they want to make a complaint. This gives the illusion that customers love to complain.

Thinking about the toilet paper metaphor, it's clear that people aren't happy if something they need is done the wrong way or missing. The same frustration about the way the toilet roll hangs is common right across your business in relation to the way that service is provided (or not provided) and the way complaints are handled (or not handled). As author Jane Austen is reputed to have said, 'My sore throats are always worse than anyone's.' Customers think their issues are most important and making it difficult to complain only makes things worse.

Over time, the use of technology has made it more uncommon and hard to talk to a person. We need to provide easy opportunities for customers to give feedback in real time to a real person when something occurs. Let them know the human channel is always present, but, most importantly, make sure your frontline staff can deal with complaints at this level. Over the phone also counts as 'in-person' feedback, but it can be frustrating to wait on hold, so reducing call wait times should be a focus.

Just because social media and emails are a great tool for business, it doesn't mean that they should become the only way customers can give feedback. As a minimum, you should make sure the contact phone number is obvious and accessible on your website. The last thing customers want to do is search through lots of pages and links to find a phone number. If this is the case, it gives the impression that you don't want customers to call you. Training someone to be a 'keyboard warrior' doesn't help either. The greater delay between the problem and the complaint, the greater the chance that the customer will remember it much worse than it was. This makes the resolution part more difficult. Many car mechanics proactively reach out to customers after a service to check how the car is performing before the customer has a chance to get in touch with the service department.

QUESTIONS TO CONSIDER

- Do you make it quick and easy for your customers to give you feedback in person?
- Are frontline staff able to deal with complaints without the need to escalate?
- Can you see an opportunity to proactively follow up with your customers?

Service drives the experience

Customer service, like toilet paper, hasn't changed in years. Do you know when commercial toilet paper was invented?

In 1857, commercial toilet paper first became available. In 1871, perforated sheets were introduced. In 1879, the paper was put on a roll for the first time. In 1891, the perforated roll as we know it was patented.

Service evolved over a similar period of time. In 1868, the world's first money-back guarantee was introduced, signalling a push to focus on customer satisfaction. In 1876, the world's first electric telephone was patented, which revolutionised service, giving customers and organisations the ability to directly and more immediately get in touch with each other. In 1887, the world's first 'buy one, get one free' discount coupon was released by Coca-Cola, signalling the start of building relationships for increased purchases.

While we can date when toilet paper was commercialised and when customer service became more prevalent, the need for customer service was present long before 1868, just as there would have been a need for toilet paper long before 1857. For thousands of years, humans will have used *something* as toilet paper, and for thousands of years humans would have been providing service to one another. In fact, the oldest known written complaint was the 'complaint to Ea-Nasir' in 1750 BC.[18] It was etched into a clay tablet in a now extinct East Semitic language. Customers may have existed before then, trading in ancient Egypt dating back to the fourth millennium BC. Therefore, the concept of serving one another is not new.

While service hasn't changed, over time our perceptions of service have. If you think about some of the training programs that emerged in the late 1980s and throughout the 1990s, service became a phrase that effectively meant selling. Into the 2000s, service became about effective communication, and, today, the buzzword 'experience' seems to have replace service as the preferred word.

A few years ago, I was talking to a potential client who owned a café-restaurant. As we were discussing customer service, he told me that his café had great service as it was. He told me his focus was now on the greater customer experience and not customer service. I asked him, what sort of experience he wanted his customers to have, and he told me that because he had a high number of customers who would come in for a lunch meeting or lunch during their break from work, he wanted the café to give customers a 'quick' experience, while still offering quality food.

As we discussed it further, the owner found that the level of service was in fact the issue that was contributing to the current and undesired customer experience. For example, to have a quick experience, customers must be greeted promptly at the door. That's service. They must then be seated immediately and given a menu. That's also service. The waiter must come back in a short period of time to give the customers water and take their order. That's service too. The chefs must prepare the food knowing that customers are on short timeframes. That's service again. Finally, when the food is ready and the bell is rung, the waiters must get the food to the customers' table immediately. That's once again service.

Being of service drives most of the desired customer experience (note that user experience (UX) is something different). If you consider the experience your customers are having and if it's not what you or they expect it to be, it is highly likely the problem rests with service.

Earlier we discussed the concepts of 'old-fashioned' service and not losing this service for the sake of automation and technology. Remember the milkman who delivered milk to your door? During the Covid-19 pandemic, Brownes, the local milk provider in my city of Perth, who has been in the milk business for 130 years, relived a piece of history and brought back milk delivery direct to customers' homes.

In 2017, the OG Speed Shop, a petrol station in the Adelaide suburb of Klemzig was still putting fuel in cars without the need for the customer to get out, as well as checking the oil and washing the windscreen, a tradition that started when the service station opened in 1927. By 2017, it was one of the only petrol stations in the city of Adelaide that still offered this service.[19] This is just in Australia, but there are countries that still offer this 'full service' experience at the petrol station.

The milkman and the service station attendant are two examples of what people remember fondly about old-fashioned service that's changed over time. Buzzwords like customer experience confuse what it means to serve, and communication, while an important element of service, is not the only component.

Service is everywhere around us. New Zealand actor Sam Neill once said on the TV program *Australian Story*, 'As an actor you're there to serve the script, serve the director, and serve the story.'[20]

Service hasn't changed, only our perceptions of it have.

QUESTIONS TO CONSIDER

- Are all the individual tasks your people perform making a positive difference to the customer experience?
- Do you see customer service beyond 'effective communication'?
- What old-fashioned service do you fondly remember?
- Are there any opportunities to go 'back to service basics' in your organisation?

Same things in different ways

When you go shopping for clothes, what type of customer are you? Pick one of the following three options.

A. You want to be left alone to look at clothes in your own time.

B. You like to do most the work yourself but appreciate being checked on from time to time.

C. You want the salesperson to gravitate toward you, giving you suggestions, colour recommendations and bringing you different sizes to try.

Are you A, B or C? When I ask this, there's generally an even spread across all three options. For me, I would say option B, but there was a time when my preference changed. I went clothes shopping on the morning of my son's christening. I had realised I needed a new pair of pants and a shirt the night before. Under time pressure I rushed to my local department store and became 'customer C' from the options above. The salesperson was my hero in the moment, making sure I got my new clothes and arrived at the christening on time. Great service in this case is all about reading the room.

Even when we have a bias as to what type of customer we are, it doesn't mean we can't change depending on the situation. There are different ways we can serve our customers too.

Customer service training is a program that teaches people to serve in a particular way, but it doesn't work. A mentor of mine taught me to ask three questions when training didn't work. Either something was missing, something was misunderstood or the situation was too complex. When it comes to customer service training, typically all three apply.

There are far too many possibilities to think about when serving customers that training can't capture. The ambiguity of many of the things we need to think about in relation to service can be misunderstood, and that's before we look at the individual customer situation. This includes the customer's emotions, which can make things far more complex to deal with than the theory classroom training will provide.

At the same time, the world is full of cliché phrases around customer service. These phrases are well known but over-used. They create uncertainty and ambiguity, but are too often used in training. I've managed to string them into a sentence below:

> Let's raise the bar for service
> Because the customer is king
> We surprise and delight our customers
> By exceeding their expectations
> And going above and beyond
> As we create 'wow' moments
> Because the customer is always right!

Reading these lines is somewhat poetic and can make you feel good in theory, but it's not helpful in practice.

Although many training courses would have us believe otherwise, there is no silver bullet when it comes to cus-tomer service. If you go on a first aid course, you can learn the technique for cardiopulmonary resuscitation (CPR) and apply those exact same skills to a real-life situation. On the other hand, customer service training gives us the theory, but we still need to think about what to do in each individual situation.

The 'golden rule' used to be to treat customers as you would like to be treated. It's been more than twenty-five years since Dr Tony Alessandra coined the 'platinum rule' to 'treat customers the way *they* want to be treated',[21] but this is still not embraced by many businesses.

Ask your staff members to give you a one-word answer to this question: what do you consider to be exceptional customer service? You'll likely get a different answer from each person. Likewise, ask them to give you a one-word answer to the following question: 'What do you consider to be poor customer service?' Once again, you'll likely get a different answer from each person. Finally, ask everyone whether they disagree with any of the other answers, and they'll likely say 'no'. This means if you asked fifty people to answer these questions, you could get one hundred different answers, and every one would be right.

The one thing that every customer has in common is that they are all different. This is why service is not about doing different things but rather doing the same things in different ways. The way you empower your team members will help them be in tune with the different ways to serve each of their customers.

Customers are multigenerational and, as they go out together, service should encompass all of them. Interacting with all members of the family – including treating the children as heroes by saying 'hi' or giving them a high-five – can make a huge difference. This shows that one customer as a family can involve several different interactions.

Customers should not be segmented for the purpose of service. While they may share certain demographics in common, they are ultimately individuals and expect the service they receive to cater to their specific situation and not that of the segment. Segmentation is really useful for product design and marketing but not so much for the service experience.

As I conclude this chapter, the most important point to emphasise is that the 'myths' that are commonly spread by people who aren't service minded should not be repeated by your staff members. Completely removing these dated perceptions is the first step in making headway in the service culture.

QUESTIONS TO CONSIDER

- What was the best customer service you have ever received and what made it so good?
- What was the worst customer service you received and what made it so bad?
- Do you see any of these examples present in any service situations in your organisation?

2
Decide

Confront the elephant in the room

If you're truly going to transform your service culture, there are a series of decisions you need to make from the beginning. These decisions also act as a reference tool for you and your team so you can check in with your commitments.

Whenever I think about times when I've let something fester for too long, or not acknowledged the reality of a situation, the worse it's become. However, when I've confronted the elephant in the room, as hard as it was, I've felt better afterward.

Starting a cultural change journey like this doesn't just have one elephant in the room – it has a few. Initially, these are reservations, held entirely due to misconceptions about service. If not addressed, they can become unproductive distractions that move you further away from your goal.

It's because of these reservations that people don't typically trust a process or do the work that's required of them.

Think about navigating this journey using a compass. If you imagine the cardinal points of the compass as different directions you can take, each direction has a 'decision' that you must confront. Often people try to avoid these decisions, and as they appear in every direction, they stand still and move nowhere.

In Latin, the suffix '-cide' means 'to kill'. To 'decide' means to kill off choices or options (it comes from the same family of words as homicide). The task in this chapter is for you to make some clear decisions to 'kill' these misconceptions to successfully embark on this journey. As Mark Manson said, 'Commitment gives you freedom because it determines what is worth paying attention [to] and what is worth ignoring.'[22]

The four 'elephants', or misconceptions, are shown on the compass model. They are:

- **North**: There's Nothing New to learn about customer service.

- **West**: What's Wrong with my customer service?

- **South**: Customer service is Simple Stuff.

- **East**: This cultural journey seems a bit of an Excessive Exercise.

NOTHING NEW

WHAT'S WRONG

EXCESSIVE EXERCISE

SIMPLE STUFF

Decision Model

QUESTIONS TO CONSIDER

- Be honest with yourself, what reservations did you first have when picking up this book?
- Do you agree with any of these common misconceptions abovc?
- Would people in your organisation think the same about these reservations?

The rest of this chapter will explore the four reservations and misconceptions in detail, and, at the end of each section, you will be invited to overcome them and make a commitment for the future. Quick tip – the answer to each decision should be 'yes'.

There's always something new to learn

Moving forward is all about learning. To quote Mark Manson, in his book *The Subtle Art of Not Giving a F*ck*, he writes, 'The man who believes he knows everything learns nothing. . . we cannot learn anything without first not knowing something.'[23] It's not our fault that we think we know all there is to know about a topic.

When I tell people what I do, they usually respond by saying, 'Oh awesome, we've done all the customer service training in our company already', or 'We ran one of those training courses years ago.' Remember though, if customers are always changing then service must always be evolving too. While there are many courses on service available, there are greater depths that we can explore.

Swiss psychiatrist Carl Jung once said, 'If a man knows more than others he becomes lonely.'[24] If we think we've learned everything we know about service, we can quickly fall behind as those who continue to learn move forward.

Decision One: Am I open to learning new things about customer service?

You can always improve your service

Back to the compass metaphor. If you are heading to a destination but you're off course, even by just one degree, over the entire journey, imagine how far away from your destination you'll end up?

One of the best parts of my job is the more times I deliver training programs, the more it helps me continuously reflect on my own service. There is a belief that once we learn something we don't need to cover the same ground again, but this isn't true.

The more experienced you get, the easier it is to become complacent and slack, even marginally. It should be our duty to constantly seek out feedback and improve ourselves.

When I worked in learning and development roles, I used to hear how people were excited when sent on a leadership course. Meanwhile whenever someone goes on a customer service course, they think it's a direct attack on their customer service skills.

Once I was asked to deliver a program to an entire organisation because one person's service was poor, but the leader was not willing to have the direct conversation with them. They put the whole company though a training program with the hope that the one person would subtly get the message, while the rest of the team were thinking, 'What's wrong with my service?'

As well as being open to the idea, creating a culture of service should help you remember some of the things you've learned that you've simply forgotten. Some of my most profound moments at the front of the classroom have not been in teaching people but helping them remember things they already know.

Decision Two: Am I willing to critically evaluate my own performance in how I serve others?

Service is simple, not easy

The heading here is a bit of a giveaway, but if I asked you whether you think service is simple would you say yes?

Or would you say no, thinking it to be complex? I maintain that service as a concept is simple. It must be. Think about customer service across most industries. There's no qualification needed (although sometimes I wish there was one). You can work in customer service while at school (and sometimes I wish customer service was taught in schools). It's not like being a surgeon or an engineer, and seems to be something most people could do.

If service is simple, why on earth is so much of it still of poor quality? It's not always because the person serving us doesn't understand what good service is, they just have difficulty in actioning it. As well as that, sometimes we can struggle to get the basics right.

I recently saw a meme on the internet which talks about everything being 'hard', and that we must choose what 'hard' work to focus on. For instance, marriage is hard, but so is divorce. Keeping fit is hard, but so is obesity. Being financially disciplined is hard, but so is being in debt. To add to this, exceptional service is hard, but poor service is also hard. We must choose which hard to focus on.

If north on the compass is moving forward, from a directional point of view, to go south would be to move backward. When something is difficult it stops us moving forward and holds us back. It's important here to evaluate continuously why service is important to keep progressing forward.

Decision Three: Can we strive to get service right more often?

It's not excessive when you know why

A few years ago, I was visiting a close family member who was critically ill in hospital. As things were uncertain, I was at the hospital for hours each day. I'd chuckle to myself every night about how confronting it can be when you're emotional and you get hit with a heavy parking fee, day in and day out.

By complete chance, a few weeks later I got a phone call from the parking company at the hospital. They wanted to explore the idea of me running customer service workshops for their parking attendants. I honestly couldn't believe it. At the initial meeting with one of the managers, I asked why they wanted to run the training. The answer shocked me. I was told that it was approaching the end of the financial year and they needed to spend their budget on some sort of training. They figured that customer service training was the easiest course to run in the shortest amount of time possible. In other words, the training was to be an excessive exercise.

At the start of the program, I asked the participants why they thought the customer service training was important (even though I knew as far as the management was concerned, it wasn't). One participant raised her hand and said, 'We are the first point of contact and last point of contact at the hospital. Our customers are highly emotional, they don't want to come here, but they need to. If we have compassion in our service, we can positively contribute to the customer's experience.' Unbeknown to them, as one of their customers, I wholeheartedly agreed.

It's unfortunate that, historically, training and cultural transformation programs have been seen as tick-box exercises. As we go through this book, I can help you with the first three decisions. I can help you learn something new, make you reflect on what you can improve on and show you how to make service easier to deliver. The one thing I can't show you is why service matters to you, your organisation and your customers. I can help you, but it is up to you to understand why service is important for your organisation and customers, like the parking example at a hospital.

Regardless of why you picked up this book, it will make more sense when you can connect it to the heart of what matters to your customers. Everything has been written for a reason, and any time you read something that makes you question whether it's important or not, keep asking yourself 'why' and be open to explore a new path that you perhaps may not have considered before.

Decision Four: Can I see why a culture of service is important for my organisation?

Be prepared for distractions

You've now hopefully said yes to all four decisions. As a leader, you're committed to moving forward and those decisions were the main hurdles. The challenge is to focus on service culture while running the business.

There was a TV commercial many years ago for technology company EDS (now DXC Technology). Their tag line was 'We build your digital business even while you're up and running'. Their ad showed people building an airplane while it was flying. In a sense this is what a leader needs to do. Leading a culture of service while leading a business – but without micromanaging.

Speaking of flying, many people are surprised to learn that the moment the plane wheels are brought up after take-off to the moment they go down for landing, it's likely the aircraft will be flying on autopilot the whole time.

Sticking with this metaphor, I'd like you to think of your organisation as the plane and your customer service as the autopilot. The autopilot is responsible for the entire flight, just like customer service is what makes your business work. With autopilot, the pilots don't sit and forget about the flight. They know autopilot isn't fool proof and need to keep checking.

Equally, customer service isn't fool proof, but leaders can forget to check on it.

While the autopilot is running, the pilots on a plane perform three core functions: they make sure the plane is heading in the right direction; they continuously look at the weather to avoid bumps on the way; and they make sure everything on the aircraft is working properly. Meanwhile, the autopilot flies the plane.

The role of a pilot is similar to your role as a leader. Your focus is the big picture strategic direction – making sure your organisation is going the right way. You need to be aware of the potential bumps that could stop you doing business, and you need to make sure everything is working, such as addressing the legal issues, insurance, paying bills and wages. You are responsible for all the moving parts of the organisation.

A pilot does this but checks on the autopilot too. How often do you check on your service? Do these other tasks distract you? It's true that customer service usually works on its own, just as planes are also designed to fly on their own, but pilot error can crash them. Customers will notice if your staff are on autopilot. You as a leader must pay attention to this.

I'm sure you get the idea that service is important, but other important things will arise that can be distracting. You must keep customer service on your radar because you're in trouble if it fails and you're not aware of it. This is a defining moment that differentiates organisations that embrace service and those who don't. The latter say they are too busy for service, the former gives service a seat at the table.

There is one more bonus decision to make in addition to the previous four. If you answer yes to this one, you're ready to move forward.

Decision Five: Can service remain at the forefront of my mind despite other business distractions?

3
Discipline

Become a customer service expert

When you think about high performance and achievement, discipline is cited as one of the essential ingredients to keep focused. To stay abreast of your customers' changing needs, you need the discipline to not be either too prescriptive or loose around service in your organisation. Businessman Warren Buffet is reputed to have said, 'We don't have to be smarter than the rest. We have to be more disciplined than the rest.'

Customer service is not black or white but grey, and you'll mostly find yourself in the grey area. The problem with transforming a customer service culture is it can work too well. This is because most people can be binary in their thinking. A binary thinker is someone who takes one side of something or another – and the middle bit, or grey area, is either ignored or goes unnoticed. You're probably familiar with the analogy of something being black or white, but here are a few more binaries: right or wrong. Good or bad. Best or worst. Yes or no. Smart or dumb. All or nothing. With or against.

Through my observations and interactions with the super-market industry, I am always fascinated by the staff and their attentiveness at the delicatessen. I've noticed that if I approach the deli when it's quiet, usually a staff member will have their back turned to the counter. When I've worked with delicates-sen staff and asked them to be continuously on the lookout for customers who are waiting at the counter, their response is, 'But the manager told us to keep the meat slicer clean', or 'We were told that food hygiene is really important.' What's interesting about these points is they are completely true – the manager did say to keep the meat slicer clean, and food should be stored properly, but they never said to do so *instead* of customer service.

Just because someone is given one task, it doesn't mean that the other task is no longer important. Leaders can work on sharpening their communication, which will be explored later.

When I delivered in-house service inductions, I expe-rienced the same thing. I would mention that customer interaction was important, and would get comments such as, 'Am I supposed to keep talking to customers even while there is a queue waiting for me?' or 'How can I talk to a cus-tomer when it's busy?' The need to have customer interaction is twisted to completely ignore all other customers so as to be able to interact with just one. Or the notion to interact with a customer implies it must be a long interaction and not a short one.

It takes tremendous discipline to not go too far in each direction. Having said that, there always is an exception to the rule. In 2016, Zappos employee Steven Weinstein broke the company record for the longest customer service telephone call, lasting ten hours and forty-three minutes[25] – proving there's no barrier when it comes to service at Zappos.

A few years ago, when I was working in the leisure industry, I overheard a frequent interaction take place with the receptionist. Customers would ring up to ask the temperature of the pool. The pool wasn't heated, and continuous temperature checks were performed, but when the receptionist stated a temperature the customer would be confused and ask another question such as, 'How warm is that?' If the receptionist gave a vague response, 'The water is comfortable', the customer would question the receptionist's definition of comfortable with their definition of comfortable.

After this happened a few times, we started to explore other words to use that could help the customer understand, or at least be happy with the answer without going around in circles. We finally found the perfect word. The pool temperature is. . . 'moderate'. As soon as customers heard the word 'moderate' they were satisfied and happy to end the call. However, what does moderate mean? It means 'not extreme'. In other words, the water won't be boiling, and it won't be freezing. It's somewhere in between. Even when you're in a room with someone and you think the room is cool, and they think it's warm, you can both agree that it's moderate.

How does the word 'moderate' relate to discipline? You can be on a diet and eat junk food in moderation. You can have a night out but drink in moderation. It means when you are trying to be disciplined about something, know the parameters and don't go too far in either direction. There is a misconception that having discipline means you have to do things to the extreme.

When it comes to service, I have identified five core disciplines that are essential for most situations. The disciplines are all in the middle or moderate area, with examples of a prescriptive (high) extreme and a loose (low) extreme. The task here is to look at the extremes and identify whether you have a bias toward the prescriptive side or the loose side, and how grounded you are to the middle in life in general. How you are in your home life is likely how you'll be at work too. This chapter goes through each discipline with specific examples for each extreme, as outlined in the following model.

LOW EXTREME	DISCIPLINE	HIGH EXTREME
IGNORANT	AWARE	DISTRUSTING
PARTIAL	THOROUGH	OBSESSIVE
HESITANT	CALCULATED	CARELESS
CALM	PATIENT	ANXIOUS
IRREVERENT	SENSIBLE	SERIOUS

Discipline Model

QUESTIONS TO CONSIDER

- Do you think you are too prescriptive about serving others?
- Or, do you think you're too loose around the idea of service?

Be aware of others

Awareness is about knowing what's going on around us, so we can be more prepared for our customers. I was taught this from a young age. I remember going grocery shopping with my mum as a child, and, like all children, I'd wander away from the trolley. There would be someone else in the aisle, and my mum would call to me to watch out for others. As a child you don't have awareness when you're moving around in public, but my mum was aware.

Now I say that children don't have awareness, but this is also common in adults. For instance, if I go to the supermarket for one specific item, it's to buy a blade cartridge refill for my shaver. These seemingly small items are not cheap, and, because of the blade, they are covered in security tags. I realise I need a new one late in the evening, so I dash to the shop to buy one for the following morning. As the shop is quiet, I go straight through the self-service checkouts where there's usually a person standing on their little anti-fatigue mat. As I approach the row of checkouts, they see me but decide to wander off and collect baskets or tidy up. Sure enough, as I scan the item the light starts flashing, and I need to get the person's attention to come and bypass the security warning. This has happened on more than one occasion, and it's evident the person does not look at what I'm carrying to foresee they might need to stay put for an extra minute.

I've also found this in more professional settings such as when I approach a reception counter. The receptionist can see five metres in front but doesn't look up, popping away from the counter to file something or to answer the telephone just as I get to them. Both of these examples identify how staff members are oblivious to the fact there are customers around them who need serving.

When I finished high school, I worked in a department store and my job was to restock items and serve customers. It was dubbed 'Murphy's Law' that the moment a customer was waiting at the cash register a manager would walk by and tell me so. It seemed like bad luck, but service-focused leaders are always on the lookout for a waiting customer.

It's like cooking: if you turn your back to the stove for a minute, things can start to burn.

This is common not only in static frontline positions but also in non-face-to-face contact roles. Examples of being ignorant to others can include a lack of urgency around responding to emails or answering phones quickly, or getting to work on time to be of service. There's a saying that the same people who tailgate cars when they're in a hurry, slow down and wonder what the hurry is when others tailgate them. When it's us in a hurry we let everyone know about it, so it's important to pick up on when others are in a hurry too.

On the opposite end of extremes, staff members can be hyperaware and become distrusting. For example, when customers are returning unwanted items for refunds, staff may believe that each customer who asks for a refund is a scammer trying to commit fraud. Or they may treat each customer as a potential shoplifter. Staff members may behave like this because they've had one or two experiences of customers doing the wrong thing in the past. Therefore, they penalise all customers because of the select few. This mentality is that of 'rules are rules, and we must do everything we can do to protect the company from all of the thieves trying to take advantage of us'. In these situations, you should be aware of those who do the wrong thing, but you should not treat everyone as if they fit into this category. If you treat every customer as if they have good intentions, you might be wrong, but with heightened awareness you'll know who to trust and who not to trust.

QUESTION TO CONSIDER

- How aware are you and your staff of customers around you?

Be thorough with your service

Being thorough means getting things done properly and effectively, but thoroughness too can present as a grey area depending on the customer and their request.

In the movie *Love Actually*, Harry (played by the late Alan Rickman) is contemplating an out-of-marriage romance with a co-worker. While Christmas shopping with his wife he secretly tries to buy a necklace as a present for his love interest. The purchase doesn't happen, because he is served by the eccentric jeweller Rufus (played by Rowan Atkinson). This scene is amusing to watch as Harry wants to buy the necklace and get out before his wife comes back, while Rufus goes over the top wrapping and packing the box multiple times despite being told not to. While this is a scene from a movie, in real life there are many instances where people in service don't get the hints from customers and are too obsessed with small details.

The world is flooded with phrases such as 'be obsessed by customer service' and the clichés from Chapter 1. This sounds nice in theory, but obsession is unhealthy, and by no means should service be obsessive or over the top; it just needs to be done well.

On the other hand, there are many situations where the opposite occurs – doing something only partially. For instance, think of when a parent tells their child to clean their room before they can go out to play. The child grabs everything and throws it in the cupboard before slamming the door to stop it from falling back out again. This happens in service too.

As customers, we observe people who rush a job and know it's not done properly. When you order fast food and something is missing from your bag, when you ask a waiter to wipe your table but they miss parts, or you get a response to an email but only your first question has been answered, you are receiving partial service.

QUESTION TO CONSIDER

- How thorough are you when completing tasks for others?

Be calculated with your responses

As a child, my parents encouraged me to speak up if I wanted to say something as they knew I'd regret it if I didn't. The advice prepared me for dealing with others. They also taught me to think about what I was saying before I said it so as not to end up saying the wrong thing.

In customer service, we face a myriad of situations in a single day. Some can take us by surprise or be a trigger for us and bring out our worst. Even though it doesn't always feel like it, working with customers in a general sense is not a life-or-death situation. There is time to be calculated and think about your response and decide whether it's worth it or not.

Being hesitant is less assertive, or passive. As a customer, I have witnessed situations where other customers take advantage of the people serving them (often younger people). At this extreme, customers are like bullies, and the staff member feels too intimidated to speak up even though they are not expected to tolerate abuse from customers. This doesn't only apply to adversarial situations. Staff may also avoid telling a customer about a delay because they don't want to upset them, or they may not tell a customer additional necessary information because they can't be bothered.

The other extreme is someone who is careless with customers. There is usually at least one person in an organisation who doesn't have a filter. They are blunt with customers and speak their minds. There is a fine line between speaking your mind and being careless. Not knowing this line can get staff into trouble and cause situations to escalate unnecessarily. Being careless is not good service.

In the Netflix series *The Crown*, there is a fantastic scene where the young Queen Elizabeth, grappling with her new role as head of state, tells her grandmother Queen Mary that to say nothing feels like the easy way out. Her grandmother responds, 'To do nothing is the hardest job of all, and it will take every ounce of energy that you have.'

Serving others is not like being a monarch, but you should consider the consequences of being careless, as well as considering the consequences of being hesitant. If we can be more calculated in more situations – knowing when to speak up and when not to – the outcome is likely to be more favourable for both the customer and the organisation.

QUESTION TO CONSIDER

- Do you think before you speak and act?

Be patient with others

My parents ran their own business, so growing up there wasn't as much structure as there might have been if they had had a job with set hours. Sometimes my siblings and I would be the last to be picked up from school, and my parents would have to do more work between school pick-up and dinner. It wasn't that bad, but as a child, being picked up fifteen minutes after the rest of your friends seemed like an eternity, as did having dinner an hour later than 'dinner time'. Whenever we complained about anything relating to time, we were told to 'be patient'. Author and religious minister Joyce Meyer said, 'Patience is not just waiting, it's how you behave while you are waiting.'[26] In other words, saying you're patient and looking patient are separate things.

When you work with others, including customers, everyone has their own version of what's important and pressing to them. This means there will be situations where you must demonstrate patience. You may need to be patient when explaining something to a customer they don't fully understand. It can trigger a moralising response – you become anxious, feel superior, you get it, it's so easy – but the customer is lagging.

It doesn't need to be in what you say, it can be observed in what you do. I have witnessed staff members looking at their watch, crossing their arms or tapping their feet while they wait for a customer to find their credit card in their handbag, or the customer taps the card at the wrong spot on the card reader. Reactions to these common moments may not be done consciously, but being impatient doesn't help the situation move any faster.

The extreme opposite of being anxious is to be calm. When I think of calmness, I think of someone who is meditating in the mountains and can zone out of everything around them. While meditating is great, appearing too calm in front of customers doesn't produce the desired relaxing effect. In fact, the opposite occurs. We're taught to stay calm in stressful situations, but customers expect you to show a level of concern that matches theirs if they are unhappy about something. By keeping 'calm' you can inflame the customer further because they think you're not taking things seriously. The same goes for telling a customer to be calm. Nobody likes to be told what emotional state they should be in, yet it is common to do this. Have you ever calmed down when someone told you to 'be calm'?

Finally, if a customer is in a hurry, let them be in a hurry – adjust your pace to match theirs.

QUESTION TO CONSIDER

- Do I display patience when I need to rely on others?

Be sensible in all situations

Customers want to feel at ease around your team when experiencing your service. As we will explore throughout the book, the way you serve someone changes on a customer-by-customer basis. You've likely heard the phrase 'common sense isn't always common', but this is the time to make sure it is.

Doing the right thing for a customer is the sensible thing to do. Questioning a policy that was developed ten years ago that no longer seems relevant is the sensible thing to do. Empowering your staff to use their common sense is one of the biggest steps and often hardest hurdles to overcome.

When it comes to sense, people tend to stray toward the high extreme and become too serious. Many workplaces tell staff members to not talk to each other while serving customers (although it's still far too common to hear staff chatting about their weekend plans while serving you), but that doesn't mean when there are no customers around staff can't look like they're enjoying themselves. A serious vibe can be off-putting to some customers, creating awkward moments, and it will make the day feel like a drag – which frontline staff commonly complain about.

Being irreverent is the opposite of taking things seriously. It can be a bit cheeky, flippant and sometimes rude. This shouldn't be a deterrent, but today more than ever, there are sensitive topics that, if not taken more seriously, can land people in a lot of trouble. It's OK to have a sense of humour and make the odd joke, if appropriate, but bear in mind this will be taken differently by different customers.

The media showed much of the late Prince Philip's lighter side over the years. These were referred to as 'gaffes' and were mostly completely harmless. What it demonstrates is that even for a member of royalty, who is seen to be serious and following protocols, it's OK to have a laugh. Some of the funniest moments and television bloopers occur when people have a laugh. To laugh off every single mistake is irreverent, but customers are usually tolerant with the odd mistake and will tell you it's not a worry if you become too serious about it.

Think of the Uber drivers who started carpool karaoke with their customers. These drivers became viral hits online with many following the trend. The video compilations only show the customers who chose to sing, but it's a great example of how singing in the car – something most people do – can be used to enhance the experience of a rideshare service.

Clive James is commonly believed to have said, 'Common sense and sense of humour are the same things moving at different speeds.'

QUESTIONS TO CONSIDER

- Do I apply common sense to most situations?
- Think of a time you experienced poor service in the opposite extremes of each of these disciplines. Can you see how being more centred would have provided a better outcome for your situation?

4
Divide

Mind the service gap

Most people can recall the fairy tale story of Hansel and Gretel who were taken into the forest by their father and stepmother to be abandoned. Hansel takes a slice of bread and leaves a trail of breadcrumbs, but the children can't find their way back because the birds have eaten the crumbs. What most people don't remember is that Hansel and Gretel were taken into the forest twice. The first time Hansel (who overheard his parents talking) gathers pebbles to leave a trail so they can return. When they return, their stepmother, in rage, locks them in their room so they don't have the chance to gather pebbles again, hence they could only find bread when they were taken back the following day.

When we think about cultural change and this story, it is common for businesses to be like Hansel. Once on the journey, leaving a trail of pebbles allows the organisation to find its way back from any progress it makes. The difference between cultural change and this fairy tale is that cultural change should be a one-way journey – yet if we metaphorically leave ourselves pebbles, it's easy to turn back to the way things were.

In all cultural change journeys, a gap will form between where your organisation is now and where you want to go. It's likely this gap will be bigger than you imagined. The gap, or divide, may cause some tension initially, but once you make the giant step over, it will be a distant memory.

Let's start off simple and have a look at both sides of the divide. We will drill deeper shortly, but, for now, imagine that one side is exceptional service and the other side is dysfunctional service. Think about all the organisations you believe are widely renowned for their exceptional service – organisations that when you see the logo, the first thing you think of is customer service. Usually these are global brands like Disney, The Ritz-Carlton, Mercedes-Benz and Starbucks, to name a select few. Then, think about the organisations that are typically notorious for poor or dysfunctional service. Interestingly, here you would start to think more about industries than specific brand names. Industries like telecommunications, government departments and budget airlines as a starting point.

In examining these two side by side, what do you believe is the key difference between them? Organisations that are known for exceptional service typically concentrate on the wants and emotions that their customers have, while the organisations with poor service only focus on the general needs their customers have and highly conform to the industry stereotype. A 'want' is beyond the product or service they require. It looks to how they want to feel as well as what they hope and aspire for as a result of the product or service.

On the exceptional service side, I'd like to introduce the hotel chain DoubleTree by Hilton. This brand is globally famous for one thing: in every property around the world, whenever a guest arrives to check-in, they are given a freshly baked chocolate chip cookie. This signature service receives global praise. Why do you think that is? When I ask this question to people, I get responses like: because it's free; because it's unexpected; because it distracts them from the bill; because it reminds them of home; because it's not common. These are all correct, but there's one more that goes a little deeper.

Instead of telling you, I'll help you understand the real reason why the cookie is such a hit. What time is hotel check-in? Usually, 3pm. What event normally happens at 3pm? Afternoon tea. What do most customers want to do when they get to their hotel room? Relax. Where do customers typically come from when they arrive at the hotel? The airport. What are airlines famous for? Average food. What word could you use to describe how a customer is feeling when they arrive at the hotel? Hungry.

When you think about the two sides of service, wants and emotions versus needs and stereotypes, customers who arrive at the DoubleTree by Hilton need to check-in, but what they really want is something to eat. If the hotel can cater to the wants and emotions of the customer, while satisfying their needs (to check-in), they are offering a far superior level of service compared to the brands that only focus on the obvious or basic needs.

If we were to look at the other side, let's use a telecommunications company as an example. Imagine you need to call your provider to make a query about a charge on your phone bill. What do you think about when you call them? Long wait times, listening to the 'muzak', navigating the voice recognition, ending up with the wrong person, overseas call centres making it hard to hear, people never seeming to be trained in what you specifically need, being transferred to other people to re-explain yourself, finding some loophole in your contract you weren't aware of, being sold another plan and possibly being disconnected. These negative stereotypes are widely held about the telecommunications industry. If these issues exist when you call – even if your phone bill enquiry is solved – you will give the service a lower rating.

Now that we know the differences between the two sides, we will spend the rest of this chapter looking at the divide between them and what's needed to move from one side to the other.

QUESTIONS TO CONSIDER

- Can you think of local brands that are renowned for their service excellence?
- Can you think of local brands that are notorious for poor service?

From notorious to renowned

We often hear stories of poor customer service that stick in our minds, but we often overlook the many positive stories of exceptional service. This is because organisations are commonly known for poor service based on their industry, and because industries typically conform to a particular stereo-type. While there are only a few global brands that can truly claim to be renowned for their exceptional service, it demon-strates that it is possible.

There is also the misconception that the organisations with the monopoly that offer notoriously poor levels of service don't need to improve because there is no better alternative for their customers. In fact, some of the best companies have the monopoly in an industry because of their focus on cus-tomer service, like Disney and the few mentioned earlier.

This book is not trying to make your company 'be like Disney', and I promise that I won't be giving ideas that require the 'Disney budget' to achieve them. I am giving you what you need to stand out in your market from a service perspective. Sure, you may become famous like Disney one day, but the goal here is to make more people think of service when they think of your brand.

One of my favourite speeches was by US President John F Kennedy in 1962, when he said, 'We choose to go to the Moon.'[27] In under eighteen minutes, he outlined his plan to land a man on the moon. News website *Business Insider* recently took his speech and collated some of the most pro-found lines and put them together in a two-minute read. Here are the final few lines:

> 'But why some say, the moon? Why choose this as our
> goal? And they may well ask, why climb the highest
> mountain? Why thirty-five years ago fly the Atlantic? We
> choose to go to the moon. We choose to go to the moon
> in this decade and do the other things. Not because they
> are easy but because they are hard. Because that goal will
> serve to organise and measure the best of our energies

and skills. Because that challenge is one that we're willing to accept. One that we are unwilling to postpone. And one we intend to win.'[28]

If you replace the words 'go to the moon' with 'be renowned for our service culture' above, would this be an inspiring goal for you and your team? Is this the reason you picked up this book? If JFK could outline plans to put a man on the moon, this could inspire you to outline plans to make your organisation renowned for its service culture.

If you imagine any journey that's unknown, you need directions. It's no use having the starting point and end point without the turn-by-turn street directions. Likewise, it's no use saying you'll move from dysfunctional service to exceptional service – from one side to the other – without knowing the specific steps along the way. We also need to ascertain where your organisation is sitting currently. You may already be further along the journey than you think, and many organisations find themselves somewhere in between.

Looking at the following model, the first two columns (from left to right) show a list of seven levels from bottom to top, negative to positive, with words describing how your customer may feel about your service and how you would describe your culture. If you could pick a level that matches both how you think customers feel about your service and how you feel about your service culture, where would you be at? Does the word in the left column line up with the word you selected in the middle column? It's common for people to overestimate the left column and underestimate the middle column, so if there is a difference, look for the middle point between the two. Let's keep that as your starting point for now.

CUSTOMER FEELING	SERVICE CULTURE	BUSINESS FOCUS	
RENOWNED	EXCEPTIONAL	MAINTAIN	WANTS & EMOTIONS
RECOMMENDED	GREAT	MEASURE	
REGULAR	GOOD	MULTIPLY	
RESERVED	AVERAGE	MOBILISE	
RELUCTANT	HAPHAZARD	MOTIVATE	NEEDS & STEREOTYPES
REJECTED	POOR	MEDIATE	
REPULSED	DYSFUNCTIONAL	MODIFY	

Levels of Service Model

QUESTIONS TO CONSIDER

- Can I describe the level of customer service in my organisation?
- Can I describe the service culture inside my organisation?

Break away from the stereotype

By breaking down the levels of service and levels of culture, you have more manageable steps to move from one side of the divide to the other. The third column introduces the activities that you as a leader need to undertake to progress to the next level up. If you do the right thing at the right time, you will progress faster. Doing the wrong thing at the wrong time will waste time, energy and resources as it will give the illusion you are higher than you really are.

A 2005 study titled 'Advocacy Drives Growth' by the London School of Economics, reported the phrase 'more good is good, less bad is better'.[29] The report outlined that the growth of an organisation could be predicted by less negative word of mouth, rather than on positive word of mouth alone. Applying this to the previous model, there's no point focusing at the very top (although it may be tempting to) if there are things lurking below that will drag your service and culture down.

You can also see on the far right-hand column that the two sides we discussed earlier, needs and stereotypes, and wants and emotions, break up the bottom half and the top half. My goal is to get you to the very top of the top.

Regardless of where you've assessed your organisation to be at, it is useful to look at the bottom half. True exceptional service occurs when it disrupts the existing negative stereotype. It is important to at least consider whether there is a negative stereotype of your industry or organisation – and, if so, is your organisation confirming to it or disrupting it.

Stereotypes are easily formed in both industries and professions due to unconscious bias. 'Unconscious' means that it's not intentional, yet it's still very easy to make assumptions about people and customers until these assumptions become part of the DNA of the organisational culture. The term 'mansplaining' (where typically a man explains something to a woman in a condescending way assuming she has no knowledge about a topic) is just one example of what can happen when a stereotype is formed.

Earlier I shared the story about the DoubleTree by Hilton cookie. Generally speaking, industries like hotels, especially luxury ones, are more inclined to focus on the wants and emotions of customers rather than conforming to the needs and stereotypes of the industry. There has been a push over recent years for industries which are typically hovering below the line to take a stand and break away from their negative stereotype.

In 2010, the ANZ Bank in Australia launched the TV campaign 'We live in your world' with a series of popular commercials. They featured comedian and actress Genevieve Morris who played Barbara the bank manager. Each commercial focused on a customer having a negative interaction with Barbara, who completely conformed to the negative stereotype of an out-of-touch bank manager, before contrasting this to the level of service at ANZ Bank. In one interaction, the customer complained to Barbara about her bank account fees, when she was told there would be 'no monthly account fees'. Barbara's response was 'Ah, yeah, you see, when I said no monthly account fees it was "know" with a silent "k" – as in, you may not *know* about the fees until the fees are charged. Your mistake.'

While highly entertaining, there was a truth to the commercials about how banks had fallen far into the negative stereotype, compared to decades ago when the bank manager would know your name and visit you at home. Think of how banks not trusting you to not steal their pens, chained them to the counter, while expecting you to trust them with your money. In Barbara's response, the 'no' versus 'know' line shows the stereotype of hidden small print aimed at confusing customers.

It has been over ten years since these commercials first aired, and if you look at bank branches in Australia, most are no longer a sterile environment with a row of tellers. Now, they are brightly lit, with couches to sit on (not uncomfortable waiting room chairs), and a concierge desk to greet people.

What does this remind you of? A hotel lobby. We can look to other industries to help us break free from the stereotype and hotels can give us the best ideas.

In 2017, Qantas was inspired by hotels and offered passengers in their first class cabin a 'pillow menu' where they could select from three different types of pillows based on their comfort needs. This is a common practice in many hotels.

This trend has continued with Western Australian-based bank Bankwest using the slogan 'Bankwest, bank less. Less jargon, less about us, less bank stuff' while also developing their first terms and conditions document with pictures.

It's important not to get too distracted in trying to be like a hotel. Even though your service focuses on the wants and emotions of customers, you still need to address their basic needs. For instance, the customer who arrives at the DoubleTree by Hilton and receives a cookie but has a delayed check-in will certainly not be impressed with the service received, so the basics need to be addressed first. The room needs to be clean and comfortable; the cookie is the bonus.

To further assist in ideating new product or service offerings, the Kano Model, developed in the 1980s by Japanese professor Noriaki Kano is a great tool to use here.[30]

You can also take the levels of this journey and align it with a simplified version of Maslow's hierarchy of needs. At the bottom there is safety. Customers expect they will get what they need from you and feel safe in doing so. For example, an airline needs to safely transport you to your destination. The service element above the line focuses on the psychological needs like belongingness (something Apple heavily focuses on – you're either Apple or Android) and esteem (you're made to feel great whenever you walk into an Apple store).

Telecommunication companies have had bad reviews in terms of their stereotypes. In response, Australian telco

Telstra announced that within eighteen months, 100% of calls from Australian customers will be answered in Australia.[31] They have now brought back their call centres from overseas to Australian shores. Being enticed by cheaper labour abroad to handle complaints and technical questions from customers demonstrates a lack of investment in people and a lack of value placed on service. The pressure has been mounting for some time on these industries, which are finally starting to change.

It's not just about Australia versus overseas. Local insurer RAC based in my city of Perth on the west coast of Australia has advertisements that don't mention the products but concentrate on how their call centres are local and not housed in the larger eastern state cities of Sydney and Melbourne, where most companies are headquartered. The most popular commercial focuses on a couple with damage to their car who manage to call out to the insurer, claims manager and repairer who are all in their front yards of the same street – highlighting the fact they are local.

I recently went to have the tyres changed on my car. As I was waiting for the work to be completed, I noticed they had their promises printed in large font on their wall which I have rewritten here.

> We won't carry out any unnecessary work. . . ever. When we say it'll be ready in an hour, that's because it will be. We use good quality tyres and parts because they work better. No hidden charges ever. . . not even small ones. All our technicians are fully trained, so they're not just fitting fast, but right too. Any questions, big ones, small ones, silly ones, don't be afraid to ask.

Notice how each statement is promising something different to what the negative stereotype of car services centres would be. This is a great example of a heavily stereotyped industry taking a stand and making a positive difference in their service.

QUESTION TO CONSIDER

- Am I aware of the negative stereotypes that may exist about my industry and profession?

The seven levels of service excellence

The final section of this chapter will take you through each of the seven levels, from notorious to renowned, as introduced earlier in this chapter. It will cover how to know what level your organisation is at, and what your key focus as a leader should be to progress to the next stage.

1. Modify anything which is dysfunctional or repulsive to your customers

Sitting at the very bottom is dysfunctional. This is an area you want to move away from quickly because if you have a dysfunctional culture, you're likely repulsing your customers from going anywhere near your brand.

To drive someone away from interacting with your brand you need to understand what typically causes distaste or aversion in the potential customer's mind. Have a look inside your organisation to see whether at any microtouchpoints this is happening. Market research can help.

Search for examples of customer experiences that have gone particularly wrong. Typically, these are in the form of hurtful comments being made to customers. Clothing stores that shame people because they don't look like the type of customer that should be shopping with them is one example of this. If your service is dysfunctional, your customers are like butterflies, and your staff members are scaring them away.

Your focus for this is to modify immediately. Take a fresh approach. There's usually nothing to 'fix' here. You may simply have the wrong people who shouldn't be with you on this journey. As a leader, you must draw a line in the sand.

2. Mediate anything that makes customers reject doing business with you

At this level, it could be that the customer thinks the service they received was poor and rejects doing business with you in the future. Is your organisation losing customers?

Looking at the customers you once had but who are no longer yours is a good place to start if you want to figure out why they were put off. Also think about times when you rejected an organisation due to poor service. Was it because they hadn't got back to you or answered the phones, or they took too long to get back with an email acknowledgement?

We would like to think that most customers can tolerate a one-off poor service experience, but many customers won't. One in three customers will walk away from a brand after just one negative experience.[32] Would you give a business a second chance after a poor service experience?

The good news is, if you are in this level, improvement is possible. Mediate immediately with your team. Sit them down and talk to them about what isn't working as well as it should. Try to seek their agreement on the issue and their commitment to improving their service, so you can get them focusing on the things causing customers to reject your business.

3. Motivate your team when service is haphazard

Many businesses find themselves at this level despite doing some things right. If you look at your own service experiences, it is likely you are doing business reluctantly with some organisations too. This may be because you have no choice or because the alternative is no better.

If I asked you to list the things that you need to do but don't want to, you're likely to think about going to the bank, the post office, any government department or calling your phone provider. The level of service isn't helpful or is memorable for the wrong reasons. They get done what you need them to do, but, depending on the day or depending on the person, you might receive a different level of service. Because of the stereotypes discussed in the previous section, you will think of them all as the same until a new disruptor comes in and gives you a better alternative.

This stage is about motivation. Clearly things are moving in the right direction – you're kicking some goals – but everything else is missing. There's nothing radical to change here, perhaps a misalignment of one or two things that need to be tweaked. Capture the things that aren't working and motivate your team around it. It could be something as simple as ensuring every customer is taken to an item, rather than pointing them down an aisle and making them find what they're looking for on their own.

Motivation is important here because there are likely to be longstanding habits imbedded in the culture that will make it difficult to change. The work we've done on stereotypes can help you, but sometimes we can be blind to the things that are in front of us, which is why we should look at our industry from an objective point of view.

4. When service is average your customers will be reserved

Even though we are at the halfway point, there is a negative connotation with the word average. No one likes to be told they are average. A child receiving their school report with the word 'average' written on it is not looked favourably upon, yet on a business level, this is something to watch out for. If you've moved up from a lower base, all the hard work performed up to this point gives the illusion that you can rest on your laurels, but it doesn't stop here.

From your customer's perspective, being reserved can go either way. They're unlikely to bother to complete a survey from you or give you a review. Nothing bad has happened, but neither has anything been worth noting. Their views on your people are that they are doing their jobs. They remain reserved on an opinion but also reserved on an alternative.

It's a deceptive stage, as there is a misconception that customers are happy because they are quiet, which is not always a good thing. It's important to know which customers wish to be left alone, and which need attention. A great example is seen in the property management industry. Some owner-customers have complete faith in the property manager and don't need to be bothered; others want to know about the micro details of their property and be kept informed as often as possible.

As a leader, the biggest challenge here is to resist the temptation to make bold moves even though you're at the halfway mark. There is a chance that things could drop backwards, so here it's important to mobilise others. Get everyone together, share the successes, and look for the little positive and incremental changes that you can make every day that slowly set the standards higher. Anything positive here is worth celebrating. Getting someone external in who can see things that might be overlooked can really help here.

5. Good service and regular customers need to multiply

Repeat business and regular business are two separate things. Repeat means more than once, but regular means more than once with a defined pattern.

A regular customer gives the illusion they are a loyal customer, but this is not the case. Regular customers could be 'reluctant' customers. They may only be accessing your service out of convenience, because there is no better option or because the effort to use somewhere else is too hard.

American hospitality consultant Jon Taffer said that if a customer visits your restaurant the first time and has a flawless experience, there is a 40% chance they will visit a second time. If they visit your restaurant a second time and have a flawless experience, there is a 42% chance they'll visit a third time. If they visit a third time and have a flawless experience, there is over a 70% chance they will come back a fourth time, and so on.[33] The point here is to strive for four visits, not only one. The subtle point is to get the customer to come back one more time, each time, to get to a fourth time.

Author Jim Collins said, 'Good is the enemy of great',[34] and at this point you will feel some good momentum throughout your organisation. As things are going well, it can be hard to think about how things could be any better from here.

About ten years ago I was working at an organisation as their head of guest experience. We had embarked on a significant cultural change journey that took a number of years.

By the time we reached the fourth year we started to feel a different level of momentum, and the CEO and I discussed where to go from here. We identified a program run in Orlando, Florida, by the Disney Institute, and I was sent to the US for a week to be inspired and bring my learnings back. When I returned, things started to accelerate quicker than before.

I reflect on the timing of the course and wonder what would have happened if I had been on the program four years earlier. I would possibly have been overwhelmed instead of inspired and unable to identify or make the changes needed. Many businesses' transformational programs expect you to be at a certain level before you enrol with them, as the chances of success are a lot stronger if you're already making progress.

The most important advice here is to multiply what's working and take that up a notch. Australian major supermarkets Coles and Woolworths have been fighting for customers in recent years by introducing little collectables, which have become a craze among children (and their parents). When rival supermarket Aldi was asked whether they would join in on the craze, they said: 'We are very focused on anything that adds cost and complexity that could jeopardise our business model. . . we will only do what customers appreciate and see value in.'[35] Don't get distracted by ideas and initiatives that will take your business in the wrong direction.

6. Measure the great service that your organisation delivers

Imagine you're at a barbeque on the weekend and you're chatting with some friends. You'll typically be talking about anything and everything, and you may share the positive or negative stories about your week. Stories that start with 'you wouldn't believe what happened to me this week. . .'. The stories of positive service often come out unsolicited here.

Your friend might also ask if you know any good plumbers. Here is your chance to recommend someone you've had a positive experience with. The more you look after your regulars, the greater likelihood they will recommend you. Think about the times when you've acquired a customer through a recommendation and how easy it was.

This is a good point to start measuring how many new customers you're getting and whether they have been referred to you by others.

It doesn't end here – because of your progress and momentum, it will be easier here compared to previous stages to start setting team targets. This is where businesses can focus on improving their Google Review scores, TripAdvisor ratings or the number of positive compliments received. Setting targets earlier on in the process can be too ambitious and unachievable.

Be mindful of the biases that can develop here. Don't get caught up on which customers are likely to recommend you and which ones aren't. The best thing to do is ensure you are providing exceptional service to all your customers.

Delta Airlines recently shifted the way they treat their economy class passengers as well as focusing on passengers in the business class cabin. When they were asked why, they simply said there are more economy class passengers than business, which means there are more mouths that can offer positive words to others. An economy class passenger flying with their family on one trip may be a business class passenger flying alone on another.

Author and strategic adviser, Shiv Singh, is thought to have said, 'The purpose of business is to create a customer who creates customers.'

7. Maintain an exceptional service culture so your organisation stands out from the rest.

You've reached the top, now make sure you can maintain it. The best measure of cultural change is not the organisation that achieves it, but one that can sustain it in the future, and sustain it as they navigate the new complexities that business and customers throw at it.

Think about a time you chose a particular place to take your family and friends and you say, 'It's supposed to be great' or 'I've heard it's great'. You can't think of specifically who told you, maybe no one did. Or maybe someone told you based on hearsay from someone else. There are many people that have never been to Disneyland or The Ritz-Carlton, but you know the service is supposed to be amazing there. The same applies to prospective employees. If people apply for a job with you because 'you have a great culture', this is a good sign that positive word of mouth is spreading. When you reach this point, you'll know it. Leaders who are in tune know what people are saying about their brand. If they're not saying anything, you'll know you're not here yet.

Notice how I haven't mentioned service as surprising. You don't get to this level and surprise customers with how good your service is. You confirm to your customers that you're as amazing as they thought you were.

It is easy when things are going well to ignore potential threats. It takes a lot of work to stay at this level of service. If, for some reason, another player or a change in the market were to threaten this, you will be in a far better position to respond if you go back through the third column of the Levels of Service Model and determine what you need to do as a leader to stay at the top.

Looking back at all the levels, the top may seem ambitious and audacious, which is good. There is a temptation for leaders to feel that the top isn't necessary and as long as the company is in the good or great level, that's enough.

That's exactly the mentality that American print and digital company Xerox had in the 1990s. In polling customer satisfaction on a scale from one to five, Xerox had a goal to have 100% four-star (satisfied) and five-star (very satisfied) ratings by the end of 1993. In 1991, it found that customers who gave five-star reviews were six times more likely to make another Xerox purchase than customers who gave four stars. Xerox shifted its focus to achieve 100% five-star reviews by the end of 1996.[36]

While being close to the top can be good, imagine how being at the very top will be for your customers, your people and your organisation. It is my hope that you agree the top level is what you will aim for. Anything less than this isn't good enough and would not be equivalent to the moon that JFK wanted to reach. Once you commit to this, you need to be prepared to go all in. Half in won't work.

PART TWO
ENCOURAGE

5
Define

The four axes of culture

The term 'culture' is generic, while the term 'service' is specific. My vision is for 'culture' to be something specific, and 'service' to be something generic.

I tried long and hard to avoid using the word culture in my content and programs. It seemed like such a buzzword, but the more I resisted, the more it appeared.

It wasn't so much the word culture, rather the many definitions I see and hear being thrown around. They are all great definitions, but they are not useful in a practical sense. The most common definition is that culture is 'the way things are done here' or 'what people do when the CEO leaves the room'.

Coming back to my resistance to buzzwords, I realised that culture isn't a buzzword – it's been around for thousands of years. The only difference today is the way culture seems to be discussed.

Australian football great Leigh Matthews has been quoted as saying, 'Culture is what you blame when you don't know what's really wrong.'[37] I agree with that view because we hear people say things like, 'There's a really bad culture here', without pinpointing anything specific or useful to improve. If we're going to work on cultural change, we need to get clarity on what culture is.

On the other hand, the word service is the exact opposite. It's so specific. If you ever mention service to people, many immediately think of a receptionist or someone in a call centre. Service is used to distinguish between front-facing and back of house teams, which is also incorrect. It gets worse if you put the two words together: 'service culture'. Those who don't work at the front counter struggle to see how it is relevant to them.

While culture can be a fluffy word, there's no doubt it's important. There is the metaphor that culture is like the wind – you can't see it, but you can feel it. An absence of a good culture is certainly noticeable like a hot day with no breeze. Service is the same. It's important, and it's noticeable when absent.

Santa Clara University professor David Caldwell defined culture as, 'The invisible glue holding organisations together', but he also said that, 'Few people argue that building a healthy culture sits high on an organisation leader's priorities.'[38] Feeling culture is one thing, knowing that it's important is another, but doing something about it is a whole new story.

The same applies with service. I spoke earlier about customer service training not working and have seen organisations repeatedly throw money at sending their receptionists on customer service courses with little result. Service is much bigger than the receptionist, but that doesn't mean the receptionist isn't important. You need to make sure the receptionist is setting the tone, which is why they are often given a fun job title as the 'Director of First Impressions'.

If you want to fix service, you must fix the culture. If you want a good culture, it must be a culture of service. These two go hand in hand. You can't work on one without the other.

The problem is that cultures by their definition are fixed and typically don't change. If you think about any culture in the world, it developed slowly over time and it can't be easily broken. It's the same in business. It's likely that the culture of your organisation can't simply be changed. That's why this book will explore the little changes in your organisation that can collectively change the culture.

It's time to propose a definition of culture. To do this, I'm going to introduce the four axes that make up culture, which are shown in the following model. They are individuals, teams, internal and external. The definition is: Culture is where individuals come together as one team and unite over the things internal to them, and how they display these externally.

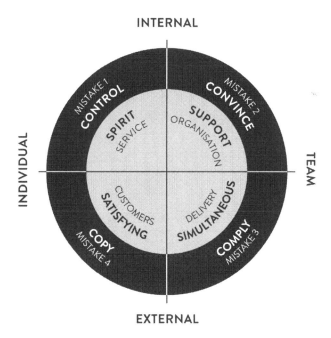

Culture That Serves Model

As you look at the four axes, you might start to make sense of the areas you need to focus on in your organisation.

- Do you have some great individuals who are excellent at working on their own, but they're not so good in a team environment?

- Do you have a great team but a few individuals that let everyone down?

- Do you have people who perform well externally, but their hearts don't seem to be in it?

- Do you hear great things behind closed doors (lip service), but it doesn't seem to translate into actions?

It can't be any simpler than that. You can have a great team, but that team must work well together. The individuals within that team must also work well when executing their individual service delivery. When all this comes together, your business must perform as a team, but the team is ultimately made up of individuals. When you have a good group of individuals that work well as a team, you've got a good culture. When you can get alignment of hearts and minds and ensure these translate into actions, you've also got a good culture.

Here is an example to illustrate this. In around 2012, a group of musicians came together and recorded a cover of Gotye's song, 'Somebody that I used to know'. The video, which went viral, showed five individuals singing and playing the music using the same guitar. They managed to have one or both of their hands on a different part of the guitar and would play their part while singing the lyrics. The way they are able to do their part individually while bringing their musical talents together is exactly what a good culture looks like.

A culture that serves

We've just defined culture, but service also has many cringe-worthy and unhelpful definitions such as 'the action of helping' or 'doing work for someone' (eye roll). Since the two are related, we need to define what a culture that serves looks like.

These cultures consist of individuals with a *spirit* for serving others, who *support* the organisational cultural direction and *simultaneously* serve in a way that's *satisfying* to others. These form the inner circle of the model.

Using these four key words, a culture that serves should be like harmony in music. The *spirit* is the non-physical part of the music. The harmony *supports* the melody – it's never in disagreement with it. The harmony is the sound made by *simultaneous* notes in a chord, and it's the harmony that produces the *satisfying* sound.

Like the four axes of culture, you're able to look at these four words and ascertain whether service is part of your organisational culture.

- Do your people have a spirit for service at their core?

- Do your people support the efforts made to improve service within the organisation?

- Do your people simultaneously deliver service across all touchpoints and departments?

- Do you hear enough to indicate your customers are satisfied by the service they receive?

If your team members don't have a spirit for service, it's likely they'll think of their work as 'just a job'. They're unlikely to support any improvements in service if they partake in gossip about customers behind closed doors. Service won't be simultaneous if you have haphazard service across certain departments and touchpoints. Finally, if you're not hearing enough compliments or good news stories, their service isn't satisfying your customers. If your team are only ticking these boxes when you or other managers are around, at least you know they can do it, but they need to work on it all the time.

QUESTIONS TO CONSIDER

- Is service a deep quality within me?
- Do I truly get on board with efforts my team make to improve culture in my organisation – I don't stand in the way?
- Do I work well with others and lead with service when dealing with my own stakeholders?
- Do I hear positive feedback about my actions?

The common mistakes

Defining culture, and a service culture, is the first part of transformation. The second part is doing what's required to make the transformation work in your organisation.

While leaders have good intentions, many of the intuitive approaches to fixing a service culture can be unproductive and do more harm than good. It's important to understand the vision but also to be aware of the potential mistakes that can be made along the way.

It's clear from the axes of culture definition that we have four areas to focus on: individuals, teams, what's internal to a person and how they display it externally. Each area has pitfalls, which are the reasons why people say that they've tried to improve their service culture, but it simply hasn't worked. They all begin with the letter 'C' and because there are four of them, I call them the C4 explosives to a culture of service: control, convince, comply and copy, as shown in the outer circle of the model.

Are you making any of the following mistakes? We want our individuals to fit in, so let's tighten our control over them. We spend all day convincing everyone that service is important. We create service polices and processes that force people to comply. We copy what other organisations do to please our customers more. All these practices seem like the intuitive thing to do, but we must think counterintuitively if we're to make any real progress.

Every day, there can be hundreds if not thousands of interactions taking place between your staff members and customers. It's impossible to control any of them. Controlling our people doesn't make them feel comfortable. They will feel like they're being cloned, and they can't provide service in a natural way. We need to be less controlling and more empowering.

There is an ancient Chinese saying that 'logic can convince but only emotion can motivate'. Think about a time when someone has tried to sell you something; the more convincing they do, the more you push back. Or think about a time you've been unhappy with a decision you've made. No amount of convincing yourself changes what's been done.

Having policies and procedures that force people to comply is a great intention. It seems to work in other areas of the business, right? Unfortunately, a health and safety policy or a bullying and harassment policy is not the same as a customer service policy. Following health and safety directives as well as standards of conduct in the workplace eliminates grey areas, which is why they work so well in a policy. As we've already discussed, customer service is full of grey areas, so it's likely that any policy or procedure you create won't work all the time. If it doesn't work all the time, it will hardly be used or taken seriously. Service is the stuff that's not in the employee handbook, and it shouldn't be.

Benchmarking other organisations can be useful. The corporate training arm of the Disney Company, called 'Disney Institute', is built on taking time-tested advice and helping other organisations and industries achieve success in the Disney way. We discussed earlier about looking to other industries to help you break free from your negative stereotypes as well. The biggest trap that this creates is it gives the illusion that you can simply 'be like Disney' or 'do what the DoubleTree by Hilton does'. Even if you're another hotel, simply copying DoubleTree and giving your guests cookies will feel clunky and forced at best. You've got to take the inspiration from other industries and make it work and feel like it's meant for your organisation.

Global industries can be a great place to get inspiration because they are well known, but the secret can also be found in some smaller industries in your local area, or industries that have nothing to do with your core product or service but can spark ideas about things that they're doing to serve their customers better.

The depths of service

Service has traditionally been seen as the function performed by frontline teams. Answering telephones and scanning groceries is considered service. This is service but only a superficial type.

The best way to think of service is like the Mariana Trench. The Mariana Trench lies in the Pacific Ocean roughly between Japan and Papua New Guinea. It is the deepest oceanic trench on earth, and its maximum known depth is just under eleven kilometres.[39] We spend most of our time swimming in the upper parts – we don't go too deep. Our approach to service works the same way. We've been operating at the very top layer, which I call the superficial layer of service, which is why we think of service as something specific.

Herb Kelleher, one of the cofounders of Southwest Airlines, first used the now popular phrase, 'Hire for attitude, train for skill'.[40] Its use has become mainstream in the HR industry today, which basically states you can train anyone the skill required to do their jobs, so don't spend too much time hiring people for their skillset if they don't have the right attitude.

Skill is how well you perform something externally, and your attitudes are the beliefs you hold internally. Using the depths of service, skill would be at the very top (the most superficial layer), and attitude would be deeper.

While Herb Kelleher is correct with this premise, I think we can take it a little further, as there is something missing. First, what comes before attitude, and secondly, what comes before skill? The missing words are character and behaviour.

Skill is how well you perform, behaviour is how you act, attitude is what you stand for and character is who you really are. These are layered as depths in the following model. All four are equally important and build on each other to come together.

SUPERFICIAL	**SKILL** HOW YOU PERFORM	**DO**	**FORCED**
SURFACE	**BEHAVIOUR** HOW YOU ACT		
SHALLOW	**ATTITUDE** WHAT YOU STAND FOR		
SUNKEN	**CHARACTER** WHO YOU REALLY ARE	**BE**	**FREE**

Depths of Service Model

Think of a famous person, living or dead, whom you admire, then think about why you admire them. People generally pick a film star, a singer, a sports player or a politician. While there is no wrong answer to whom you picked, using the table, why did you pick that person?

For example, someone might pick retired tennis player Roger Federer. When I ask why they selected him, they might say, 'Because he's one of the greatest players of all time', thus focusing on his skill. Others might say, 'Because of the way he conducted himself on the court', thus focusing on his behaviour. Some might say 'Because he fights for equal pay for female tennis players', thus focusing on his attitude. Finally, people may say they chose him, 'Because of the Roger Federer Foundation and his charity work', thus focusing on his character.

The same can work in reverse. People could admire former number one American tennis player John McEnroe for his skill in tennis but not admire his on-court behaviour and infamous arguments with umpires.

QUESTIONS TO CONSIDER

- Do I use moral judgement to do the right thing when serving others?
- Do I understand that not everyone has the same beliefs as I have?
- Do I accept that not everyone behaves the same way I might expect them to?

Being versus doing

When you think about service as something we do, there is no doubt that with the right amount of training, we can perform the task of service exceptionally well. Roger Federer doesn't need to have a philanthropic charity to be a good tennis player, but there is a key difference between service and tennis. In tennis, your technique is important, but it's all about sticking to the rules, no exception.

As we've uncovered in service, you can perform the functional elements of your job well (doing the work), but when dealing with customers it's not just about what you're doing, it's how you are being in the moment that counts. Sticking to rules in customer service doesn't always end in a win. The call centre operator with the highest volume of calls leaving no customers waiting is useless if there is no empathy or consideration given to how they speak to people while taking the calls. In addition, having great product knowledge but not applying that knowledge to a customer's specific situation by being oblivious to what the customer is really saying, or only thinking about a sales commission from selling a particular product is pointless.

My wife has a good example of 'being' versus 'doing' about dropping our son off at day care on two different days. On the first occasion, he had just been toilet trained at home, and my wife spoke to one of the educators on arrival to let them know and to look out for him to avoid any accidents. The educator said, 'No worries', and my wife left. The next day, my wife returned to day care and spoke to a different educator and told her the same thing as the previous day. This educator immediately stopped, knelt onto the ground and with pure excitement spoke to our son. She congratulated him and made a big fuss over his milestone.

The first educator didn't 'do' anything wrong, but the second was 'being' a completely different person in that moment and was far more reassuring to my wife and included my son as the customer (even though he wasn't paying). When you receive service deeper than skill, you can feel it.

You can easily tell that someone has been saying the same thing all day by the way it sounds or the way they act. Every job has repetitive elements to it, and the trick is to give the illusion that it hasn't. The last customer of the day should be interacted with as if they are the first customer of the day.

As time goes on, it's easy for people to get stuck in the rut of just doing their jobs. Despite Herb Kelleher's quote being decades old, there is still nowhere near enough focus on attitude, other than people simply agreeing with and using Kelleher's statement as a cliché.

This is the moment where we push the definition of service to be something generic rather than specific. If service can be everything about a person, not just the task they are performing, we will start to see a shift to better service globally. As French writer Antoine de Saint Exupéry is alleged to have said, 'If you want to build a ship, don't drum up people to collect wood, and don't assign them tasks and work, but rather, teach them to long for the endless immensity of the sea.' If we can look deep within an individual and bring out their best in front of our customers and teach them what they need to do, their service will fall into place.

The late Queen Elizabeth II said on her twenty-first birthday: 'I declare before you all that my whole life, whether it be long or short, shall be devoted to your service and the service of our great imperial family to which we all belong.'[41] The Queen saw her role and all of the jobs she would do as a monarch as being of service – something which she carried out for more than seventy years.

Free versus forced

The longer we focus on service as being something we do every day, the more it makes it feel forced. When you ask people in customer service roles how they are, and they respond with an eye roll, 'Ah you know, living the dream', 'Another day, another dollar', or 'Can't complain, nobody listens', you know they are stuck in the forced mentality which makes every single day feel like a drag.

It always amazed me when I had my first job just how unmotivated many people were to serve, despite wanting the job. In the supermarket I worked in there was a checkout located halfway between the cleaning equipment aisle and the freezer section. There was also a large drinks fridge that made it hard to see whether anyone was working on the register or not. Given that the checkout wasn't in front of an open aisle and was hidden behind a drinks fridge, it was the most sought-after checkout because most customers wouldn't see it and the staff could slack off. The staff were randomly assigned to it, and whenever I was on it, I found my day dragged.

It's hard to not be yourself for a whole day, especially if you're in a static role like on a checkout or reception desk. The moment I saw service as a time to bring my whole self to working with customers and not focusing only on the technical and functional elements of my job, I found I enjoyed it more. Feeling forced to be of service can also be a contributing factor to burnout, something which is heavily monitored in business today.

Over time, repetitive tasks become easy, so it's natural for a checkout operator on their first day to be serious in getting the functional basics of using the register right. If the focus from leaders doesn't observe staff members once they get the basics right, they may never develop the need or confidence to bring more of who they are out in their customer interactions. This often occurs when leaders aren't service focused and when they are not present on the frontline to notice it. In Chapter 12 I'll introduce an idea that brings more of a service focus when new staff start repetitive roles like this.

Service being liberating is not about staff feeling bound by the task they should be doing but more about the difference they are making while performing the task.

QUESTION TO CONSIDER

- Can I see service as something that's liberating rather than restrictive?

Now that we have introduced the depths of service, and distinguished between doing versus being and forced versus free, we can take these four levels of service and fit them over the service culture framework model I introduced earlier in this chapter.

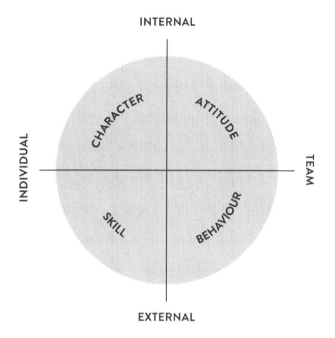

INTERNAL

CHARACTER

ATTITUDE

INDIVIDUAL

TEAM

SKILL

BEHAVIOUR

EXTERNAL

Service Harmony (CABS) Model

The character is unique to an individual, and it's something internal to them. Attitudes are held internally and can be worked on to align with teams. With the right attitudes, behaviours are displayed externally and can be standardised across entire teams. Skill is something we display externally and that each individual can learn.

The following four chapters form the most important part of the book. They will explore the four key levels of service in detail, unpacking what they are and how they should be displayed in customer service, so you as a leader can encourage this within your teams.

6
Character

The best version of you

Being the best version of yourself is a hot topic in business today. I think if we can dig deep into an individual's character and allow them to use it as they serve others, they will make an impact. This should be your goal as a leader.

Character is the moral qualities that are distinctive to an individual, the things that help us define right from wrong. Service, and in particular character, is all about doing the right thing. Think of it like returning a trolley in the car park of a shopping centre. There's no rule or law to say you should return it to the trolley bay, but most people would take the 'do it so it's not in the way of other cars' approach. A few people will ignore the unwritten rule, which is not doing the right thing by others.

If character is distinctive to an individual, and as a leader you employ many individuals, we could assume that each individual has different character attributes. Is it possible to find character attributes that are common across a whole group of individuals?

Before we look for these character attributes, it is important to distinguish the difference between character and personality. Adam Grant once said, 'Personality is how you respond on a typical day. Character is how you show up on your worst day.'[42] To expand on this, our personality is who we 'seem' to be, versus character, which is who we really are. While personalities are often easy to recognise – and still important – character is harder to recognise.

Author Helen Keller said, 'Character cannot be developed in ease and quiet.'[43] It is something that's formed bit by bit while we're growing up. As a leader, it's not something you can simply develop in an individual.

QUESTIONS TO CONSIDER

- Reflect on your own character attributes. What are they?
- Can you think of moments in your life that shaped who you are today?

The phrase 'giving discretionary effort' is a term linked to organisational performance, and it's particularly useful when it comes to customer service. We've already discussed how service is more than the task you are performing; it's how you perform those tasks. Your pay doesn't change depending on how you deliver the tasks, and we are aware that many people do the bare minimum required of them.

If you think of the greatest service you've received, an example that stands out, it is probably a time that a person has given discretionary effort. They've done something extra, something they didn't need to, because they wanted to. Most importantly, they 'did it for a cause, not for applause'. The reverse is also true. Times when people don't give discretionary service are often the best examples of poor service. When someone serves you giving discretionary effort, it reveals positive aspects about the spirit of that person, so it's worth us drilling deeper into what's inside them that makes this happen.

Let's start by looking at the three words in isolation. Giving – which means to freely transfer from one to another; discretion – which means the freedom to decide; and effort – which means determined action. These are character traits exhibited by many individuals in their life in general, not just when they are serving. It would be extremely hard to find a person who has never given anyone something freely before. It would be extremely hard to find a person who has never used their discretion to decide to do something for another. It would be extremely hard to find a person who has never applied effort and determined action in performing a task.

If we can connect people to their character traits outside of work, and bring them to life while at work, we can unite our entire workforce on these three specific traits. Why only these traits? Surely there are others? That's true, but aside from needing to draw the line somewhere, these three are the most essential for exceptional service.

If we think about times we've received poor customer service, it is usually because of the exact opposite of one or all of the above three traits. Instead of giving, the person serving you was taking something from you. Even if that something was time or your own ego. Instead of using discretion, the person serving you was being thoughtless – not considering something that mattered to you. Their inaction, lack of exertion and 'couldn't be bothered' behaviour were exhibited because it meant more work for them. Or maybe their apathy alone was enough for you to consider the service to be poor.

We must take hold of giving, discretion and effort, and stick with them because they are essential traits if we are to be renowned for our customer service culture. We started with character because our attitudes, behaviour and our skill are dependent on these three traits.

Give to others

Exceptional service should first come from an internal place of giving. I mentioned previously it would be hard to find someone who has never given in their life. Can you think of a time you've given something to someone? One obvious example is giving them a gift on their birthday.

What I love about this example is how most people never put any thought into the process of giving; it's something we just do. Here we're going to spend some time analysing what goes on for someone when they give a gift to another person, and see if we can take the same principles into service.

There are six things we uncover when looking at what goes on when we 'truly' give a gift. The word 'truly' is important as it may become apparent that people (including ourselves) may not always be giving from the heart, sometimes giving out of obligation or pressure because of cultural expectation or family dynamics. What follows is an optimist's view on gift giving.

1. Let's think how you are being in the process of giving a gift. You are fully present with the other person. You've taken time to buy a present, then you go to see the gift recipient and share maybe just a brief but personal moment with them. You wouldn't throw the gift at them

and expect them to catch it. You wouldn't quickly hand it to them as you're rushing out the door. Unless you were sending it, you wouldn't leave it for them to find on their own. You ensure that you are present as you give it to them.

2. When you give a gift, you do so without any expectation of anything in return. If you're close to them, they may return the compliment on your birthday, but the point is that you don't think to give the gift because you expect something back. Gift giving is entirely voluntary and unconditional. I find it amusing when people in business refer to giving customers a 'free gift', when a gift should be free by its definition.

3. Gift giving is a never-ending process. When around the people you care about, you buy them a present for their birthday never thinking it will be the last time you do this. If you've ever said, 'This is the last time I'm getting you a gift', it's likely you're not coming from a place of true giving anyway. The fact that giving gifts is perpetual means that you will continue to give to others throughout your life.

4. The fourth element of giving is that you're thoughtful to what the other person both needs and wants. I've received many gifts from someone that buys something for themselves, and they love it so much that they buy a second one for me. Clearly the gesture counts, but you know when someone has put a lot of thought into giving you something – most do try their hardest when it comes to buying gifts.

5. The desired outcome of the gift is a change of emotion. You want to make the person feel happier, excited or content – insert whatever positive emotion you want.

A gift has not done its job if there is no positive change in emotion.

6. The final element of giving is about you, not the receiver. Think of a time you've pulled out all the stops to buy something for someone you care about. When you find the perfect present, it excites you. You hand it over with a big smile on your face, which continues to grow as they open it and react. While you give unconditionally, what you get in return is fulfilment. You become happier when you see someone else being happy. As entrepreneur and author Jim Rohn said, 'Only by giving are you able to receive more than you already have.'[44]

Let's bring this concept of giving to the world of service. Think about the following reflective questions in relation to both yourself and the people in your organisation. Are your staff emotionally present when serving others? Are they connecting in the moment with customers, or are they just going through the motions?

Do your staff place expectations on their customers? Do they serve them only if the person does something in return? Do they expect them to get off their mobile phone, and, if they don't, make things difficult for them? When a customer is late to a meeting, does the staff member come late to the next meeting? It's not only these expectations but also expectations of gratitude. Adam Grant said, 'The point of giving is not to seek gratitude or receive recognition. . . true kindness isn't motivated by how others will react. It's an expression of who you are.'[45]

Do your staff see service as a never-ending process? Are they particularly good on the first encounter with a customer but not subsequent moments? Or are they cold when they don't know the customer well but warm up when the customer becomes a 'regular'? Are they great serving customers in the mornings or at the start of the week only to drop the standard of service in the afternoon or on Fridays?

Do your staff consider service a time to gain an insight into the individual needs of customers, or do they treat every customer the same, just like buying another pair of socks for someone every single year?

Do the customers leave feeling better than they were when they first arrived? Do your staff look at the interaction, no matter how short, as an opportunity to change the customer's emotions for the better?

How do your staff feel when they've served a customer well? Fixed a problem? Made them happier? Done something nice for them? Do they walk back into the workplace with a smile on their face or was the good service given begrudgingly.

People tell me that the hardest part of giving service compared to a gift is there is less control on how the customer will react to the service you provide. That may be true, but remember, the most important part of giving anything is the ability to let go of it – otherwise it hasn't been given. As American author Nathaniel Hawthorne is believed to have said, 'Happiness is not found in the things you possess, but in what you have the courage to release.'

This usually comes up when you give a customer advice, and they don't follow it. Once the advice is given, it's not yours anymore, it belongs to them, and they can do what they want with it. Freely giving a customer advice should never be done with the condition attached that they must follow your words of wisdom. We give the advice because we want to. It's the positive intention that counts – even if it isn't received the way you wanted it to be.

Of course, there is giving the bare minimum, and there is giving generously. The best thing about service is unlike buying an expensive present, you can be more generous with your spirit without it costing anything.

Use discretion

Exceptional service requires the use of discretion. When it comes to how you as a leader empower your staff, this is the key part. Discretion is about freely making wise and objective decisions, and comes from a place deep within an individual. Someone who uses discretion doesn't need to ask for permission. They are flexible to adapt to different situations and are great at problem solving.

Earlier, I introduced the concept of service as being something free and liberating versus forced. The use of discretion in service is one of the key components that distinguishes service between servitude and slavery. Servitude is the state of being forced to serve another person, and a slave is treated as the property of another person. These terms seem extreme here, but I have witnessed plenty of lunchroom gossip where people carry on as if their actions are that of a slave and that customers treat them that way. That's why some of the cliché phrases we discussed in Chapter 1 are not helpful. The very connotation of saying a 'Customer is King' could imply that those who serve the king are beneath them. Service is done freely, and it is discretion that makes it possible.

To serve the needs of others does not necessarily mean your own needs must come second. You need humility to know when the other person's needs are greater than your own. Discretion is what gives you the power to decide. Sometimes you need to make the decision that putting yourself first is helping you serve others better. Taking a moment's break, using breath work to be fully present and grounded, and saying 'no' to certain requests are a few examples. I call it being 'selfishly selfless'.

At the opposite end, the decisions to stay at work that little bit longer to get something done or to take lunch that little bit later than normal are taken because you know the difference you can make to another person by putting their needs ahead of yours. While service should mean a lot to you, it can mean a whole lot more to someone else.

We are exploring how character traits can be common across individuals, and like giving, discretion is also something we all possess, but many don't realise it.

Think about a time outside of your work when you have been faced with making a decision. You think about what you want, apply your conscience to it and you freely decide. We do this all the time in our personal lives; for instance, when our alarm goes off in the morning, do we hit snooze or get up straight away?

We can assume our staff will make decisions too, but there is an element of doubt about this when it comes to serving customers. This doubt exists because traditionally staff members are rarely empowered to decide what to do in any situation. When there is a lack of empowerment in an organisation, leaders tend to assume that employees can't make correct decisions.

A sole trader or company owner can make decisions easily when they are the only one involved. It becomes more complicated as the business grows, and the best thing a leader in a growing business can do is to recognise their own limitations in making all of the decisions early on and empowering their team.

Deferring to someone else to make the decision, even if the customer is happy about the outcome, loses the power and momentum it would have had if the staff member made the decision themselves. Think about how a customer feels while waiting for a manager to arrive to decide the outcome. Even if it's positive, the moment where the most impact could be created has passed.

Situations that require discretion often come without warning. Sometimes your staff will inadvertently make a promise to a customer that might not be in line with standard procedure yet is the right thing to do. A key element of service is to always do what you say you'll do, so in this instance keeping a promise should force the use of discretion without having to defer to a manager.

Everyone has discretion, and everyone seems to understand it, but there's a reluctance to use it if there is a lack of empowerment, leadership buy-in or commitment across the whole organisation. It's not only a question of whether people are empowered to use their discretion, but the environment must also be safe to do so.

Discretion is not a direct attack on rules and regulations, and, most importantly, the laws that exist. Most people don't have a problem with regulation, but when complying with the regulation creates more effort, then problems can arise.

At school we are taught to follow the rules, but, in the workplace, it's not about breaking the rules, it's about knowing how far to bend them or how to navigate around them. Rules (known in the workplace as policies and procedures) make sense in theory but are rarely guaranteed to fit into every single customer's situation.

The best service moments are like the official line review on a tennis match. When the computer zooms in to see that a fraction of the ball was on the line and the umpire makes a call and the crowd roars and cheers, that's like pushing the boundaries with discretion in service situations.

A few years ago, I was watching the Australian kids' cartoon *Bluey* with my niece. In the episode 'Shadowlands', the characters have to move around the park by stepping only on the shadows and not in the sunlight. Every time the game gets tough, one of the characters, Coco, says she wants to change the rules, so she doesn't lose. Bluey tells her she can't keep changing the rules, and by the end of the game she realises, 'You can't change the rules because the rules make it fun.'[46]

Speaking of kids, some restaurants strictly enforce the age of a kid's menu, challenging the age of a child. The point of a kid's menu is to have a smaller portion for a child – a child is a child, and the age of a child does not necessarily mean they will be more or less hungry. This is a time when discretion should be used.

To bend rules and use discretion, staff must be highly flexible. There's a term given to a person who delights in being unhelpful or obstructive by upholding petty rules at the expense of something more valuable or common sense. This word is 'jobs worth' (a colloquial word derived from the phrase 'I can't do that, it's more than my job's worth'). People like this can stifle a culture of service. They will require more attention from leaders to ensure they don't destroy the hard work of empowering other people to use their discretion.

Sometimes the answers are not right in front of us. I find it amusing how job adverts often ask for 'problem solving skills' but then there is no empowerment in the workplace to exercise these skills. Children have great imaginations, but for some reason this seems to fall away as they enter the work-force. The days of working like robots are over, and while the phrase 'to think outside the box' has been used to death, it's definitely underrated as this does not happen as often as it should.

The easiest way to make a head start on this is to keep a log with how many times a staff member asks for your per-mission to respond in a particular way in a scenario, and the number of times you've said 'yes'. If this happens a lot, it's because the 'rules' don't give them permission to 'think outside the box', and they need empowering to make the decision. It would be disruptive for both you and the customer to be interrupted by the same thing over and over again.

The hardest part is being able to let go. Many leaders and team members feel uneasy about the prospect of more empowerment in the workplace. It seems daunting at first, but most people will see correctly implemented empowerment as something to cherish. They will not take it for granted but will respect you for giving it to them.

If by any chance a staff member uses their discretion and makes the wrong decision, they are to likely know it. If they don't, coaching is a powerful technique you can use to help them see how a different approach would have been more useful.

The effective use of discretion relies on how it is delivered. Many people think it's about letting someone have something for free. Our family and friends don't expect gifts, but they are nice to receive. Likewise, when someone uses discretion, if it's delivered the right way, it will feel more like a gift than freely disregarding a rule for the customer's benefit. Discretion is one of the biggest keys for helping your organisation become renowned for exceptional service. Here are a few examples.

In early 2020, the Australian state of New South Wales experienced a summer of catastrophic bushfires. Residents in affected areas were getting automated text messages from their telecommunications provider that they were exceeding their mobile data usage limit. Knowing it wouldn't be right to leave customers without data in emergency bushfire zones, residents were extended additional data during this time.[47] Can you imagine how it would have looked if a family under threat of losing their home in a bushfire wasn't able to use data for lifesaving evacuation information because they'd 'reached the limit of their plan'?

The night before my wedding I stayed at a hotel called the Alex Hotel in Perth. I would be checking-out early the next day but happened to see this note in the room booklet about checkout time. 'We're a reasonable bunch when it comes to checkout time. Officially it's midday, but if you need a bit more time let us know and we'll see what we can do.' I love how different it felt to read that compared to other hotels I've stayed at.

There's a famous scene in the 1993 movie *Falling Down* starring Michael Douglas as William Foster. In this scene, William walks into a diner and places an order for breakfast. His server Sheila tells him they've stopped serving breakfast and he must order from the lunch menu. William isn't satisfied and calls for the manager to ask whether he can order breakfast. The manager says, 'We stopped serving breakfast at 11.30am.' When William looks at his watch, it's no later than 11.32am.

While this trivial scene was funny in a movie, in early 2021, a woman in the UK was left seething after missing the cut off for McDonald's breakfast and decided to call the police because it was unfair.[48] Even though this was not a matter for the police, there are probably situations similar to this happening every day where discretion isn't applied, and it doesn't end well for either the customers or the business.

Using discretion is about doing the right thing by someone else. When the culture of a business doesn't allow discretion, it's usually because profits are more important than people. In 2019, Australian banks and financial service companies faced a Royal Commission looking at misconduct in the industry. Some of the findings were obvious examples of not doing the right thing by a customer, such as charging fees to customers after their death.[49] The recommendations were released before the Covid-19 pandemic, and, with banks already playing catch-up with their customers, they strategically offered compassionate support and payment deferrals to customers experiencing hardships – because it was the right thing to do.[50]

Policies aren't necessarily implemented to punish the many because of the select few. Sometimes policies seem reasonable or can be backed at the time of writing, but in practice they don't work out. In Australia, there is a saying 'passing the pub test', which is thinking about a reasonable group of people chatting about something at the pub and whether they would agree or disagree with the policy.

Service fails where discretion doesn't prevail make the news for the wrong reasons. For example, in 2018, an Australian winery charged a customer $72 to cut and serve a birthday cake they brought with them.[51] The 'cakeage' charge (like corkage) was $12 per person for a cake that cost $10. A fee or charge may be reasonable, but in this situation it was excessive. With discretion operating here, the person serving those customers should see how ridiculous the policy looked in practice compared to on paper and decide to apply a more appropriate charge. This is not just good customer service, but also good brand and reputation management.

Policies are often not written by the staff that have to follow them, so it's normal to have criticism or feedback when something comes across as ridiculous when serving customers. Having said that, bending the rules once due to a customer's specific scenario doesn't necessarily mean the policy has to change. Using discretion once, or when required, doesn't set the precedent. The point is to look at the impact of the policy on each customer's situation.

While discretion is something that each individual exercises, a lack of discretion shouldn't necessarily be blamed on the individual. We should at least question whether it is something the organisation communicates and views as important. For example, a customer at an Australian supermarket was left furious after unpacking his shopping onto the conveyer belt only for the checkout operator to close the register because their shift had ended. Rather than being critical of the team member for a lack of discretion, there should be a focus on the leaders to ensure events like that don't happen again. In these sorts of jobs, there is usually a huge focus on clocking in and clocking out so it's no wonder why staff members don't see past this when it begins to interfere with customer service. Discretion as a checkout operator at a large supermarket doesn't come easy or naturally; therefore, this requires an organisational-wide approach to make team members comfortable in doing what's right.

The philosopher Plato is reputed to have said, 'Good people don't need laws to tell them to act responsibly, and bad people will always find a way around the laws.' Think about some of the restrictions in your organisation where your staff are not empowered to use discretion. How were these put in place? Does it punish the majority that do the right thing because of the few that do the wrong thing?

Using discretion in customer service is not an option. Every single organisation will have the need for discretion to be used even if it's not at first obvious.

QUESTIONS TO CONSIDER

- Do I see service as something completely voluntary that I want to do?
- Do I see others as individuals?
- Do I give my staff permission to make decisions when serving others?
- Am I confident my team will not take empowerment for granted?
- Do I believe my staff can be flexible when serving others?

Apply effort

When I was at school, my parents enrolled me in piano lessons. While I enjoyed having the lessons and learning the instrument, I wasn't a fan of practising during the week. My parents had to remind me, and I would do it half-heartedly. I'd make excuses not to do my practice because I had other things to do that were more important. During our usual arguments, my parents would tell me, 'It's a shame you don't put the same effort into practising the piano that you do into other things' (and then they'd list all the things like watching TV that I did so well).

Even as children, we can put effort into some things and not others. It happens as adults too. When people serve others, if they are doing it because they feel forced, they will likely put minimal or no effort into it, which is noticeable from the customer's perspective. Phrases like 'minimum effort, maximum result' are not helpful here. It's an expression that's useful when looking at labour and production of goods and not the delivery of service.

There's another saying that's been around workplaces for years and that's to 'have a work–life balance'. It's good advice and something important to maintain. The only issue is that it isn't particularly useful from a service perspective.

As we've been exploring in this chapter, our character is all about who we really are – something deep within us as individuals. We're focusing on bringing character traits that exist personally into our work in serving others.

The problem with work–life balance when it comes to service is that service should be something that exists in our work and life, not just something we have to switch on when we get to work each day. Invariably if you have to switch yourself into service mode when you walk in the door at work, there's a chance you might forget to do so. Writer and poet Kahlil Gibran is believed to have said, 'Life is all service', which captures the essence of what it means to always be switched on to serve.

If people can put effort into things outside of work, then there is no reason they can't apply this same level of effort to their service. Of course, if you're playing Snow White at Disneyland you probably aren't in character at home. Therefore, assuming our service doesn't require us to be in character, or require us to act, it should be something we can easily transition from our life into the workplace.

When we put effort into our service, we appear more determined than those who don't. It's hard to keep up the effort though, if the tasks we are performing seem menial or trivial. If we can help our staff members look beyond their daily tasks to the bigger picture and difference they are making with their customers, it will be easier to maintain that same effort. Some people put in lots of effort and get nowhere, so the effort must always be on something the customer values. This is where staff often begin to resent customers who still complain after they've worked so hard, without realising that everything they did wasn't valued or often asked for by the customer.

It's not hard to recognise that we put time in when serving others, as time is something tangible that can be counted. Giving a customer your time without putting in any effort becomes counterproductive, as in service, effort is far more valuable than time alone.

While I have suggested service is something that should always be switched on, it is OK to turn up the dial a little bit more before you start work each day. The reason why the staff room at Disneyland is known as 'backstage' is because cast members know whenever they go out into the park they are going 'on stage'.

Remembering to stop and smile before walking into customer-facing environments is a great strategy. In 2010, some American social psychologists Amy Cuddy, Dana Carney and Andy Yap published their research on 'power posing'.[52] They concluded that adopting powerful body language before an event gave increased confidence during the event. Starting with a smile may well be the answer to coming across more determined in front of customers.

Seriously consider the workload of your staff. I understand that service is one of the many tasks that they are expected to do, but it can be detrimental in the long run if you have staff members who are stressed, not because of their workload but because of the expectation to provide exceptional service. Stress should be minimised so that the service element of a person's job doesn't cause more anxiety than the job itself. We need to create an environment that isn't about all the tasks that need to be done in a day – in fact delivering good service makes the tasks almost invisible.

I love posing this question to people when I'm presenting a workshop. I ask them, 'What is my one task for today', while emphasising the word task. Nobody guesses it, usually saying things like 'teach us' and 'impart knowledge to us'. They are genuinely surprised when I tell them the task is to click through my slide deck by the end of the day. If I can run a session without making it obvious that I'm checking the time, worried about the slide number, or running behind schedule, the day will flow better for everyone.

A funeral director once told me that the delivery of a funeral is a business just like any other. The planning and the event itself are broken up into a list of tasks, with every member of the team playing a role. They identify their success in their job roles not by how well they complete their tasks but whether they can make the family and other attendees feel like they're the only people that have lost a loved one. Sure, they head to another funeral straight after the previous one, but no one would know because their tasks are never made obvious to their purpose.

When you work for a bigger company and have a larger group of employees, it is helpful to bring the phrase 'think like a customer, and act like an owner' into the business. The larger the organisation, the bigger the disconnect between those serving others and the overall impact for both the customer and the organisation. People are less likely to put in effort if they think that losing one customer won't make a difference.

I have witnessed an exchange between staff where a customer says, 'I'm never coming back here again', and the staff member responds, 'See if I care.' (The best response to this is, 'What can I do to make you change your mind?' The pride of many makes saying this a struggle, though.) Someone who doesn't own a company will never put in as much effort as the owner would, but it's useful to encourage staff to think about service as if it was their own company.

The mentality of thinking like a customer and acting like you own the company helps with applying effort and using discretion. The more effort applied, the more confidence you can create in the eyes of the customer. This doesn't mean your staff must be extraverted and confident people, it's simply the role of someone serving to create confidence in the other person.

In 2019, around 9,000 employees of travel company Thomas Cook lost their jobs after the company went into liquidation and ceased trading. The collapse stranded approximately 150,000 British customers who were holidaying overseas. Despite losing her job via a 2am phone call, Lucy Beatrice pledged to stand outside her closed shop. The twenty-three-year-old tweeted, 'Officially unemployed. Devastated beyond words. Even after us ceasing trading,

I will be at my branch at 9am to help my customers with any questions.'[53]

This is a fantastic example of effort in customer service. I certainly hope that your organisation doesn't go into liquidation, and I'm not telling anyone who does lose their job to park their devastation and work for free, but I want you to consider everything we've discussed under 'effort' and see how it applies in Lucy Beatrice's response. She didn't see a difference between work and life on that morning. She was determined to show her customers that she cared. She looked beyond the functional elements of her job and saw a greater benefit of the difference she could make to help her customers out. She treated the business as if it were her own while giving customers some confidence and hope. She wasn't doing her best, she was giving her best.

My favourite quote on effort is one widely attributed to author Betty Bender who is reported to have said, 'When people go to work, they shouldn't have to leave their hearts at home.' This level of effort is about how you are turning up for work and being aware of anything from home that you consciously or unconsciously may be bringing in with you.

Can you answer yes to each of the following statements?

- I don't need to switch on when I arrive at work.

- I come across as determined when I serve others.

- I don't find the need to be of service to others stressful.

- I look beyond my daily tasks to see the difference I am making.

- I approach service as if I own the business.

- I see service as a way to create confidence in others.

Because you care

In service we give to others, use our discretion and apply effort simply because we care. Care lies at the heart of all three of these character traits. It's not just caring about our customers, we need to care for them through service as well.

Anthropologist Margaret Mead summed up care nicely when she said the first sign of care existing was when a human with a broken bone survived.[54] This only happened because there was someone who cared enough to look after them while the break healed.

There are three points that surround care and lie at each of the intersections between giving, discretion and effort as shown in the following model.

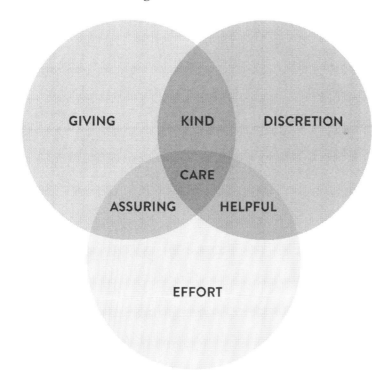

Character Model

When we give to someone and use our discretion, we are doing it because it's kind. When we use our discretion and apply effort, it's because it's helpful. When we give to someone and apply effort, it's because it's assuring to them. These three words can guide almost every decision you make when serving a customer. In any situation ask yourself:

- Is it kind?

- Is it helpful?

- Is it assuring?

All three are important because there can be situations where good service could have been great if all three were considered. Any negative service situation can be fixed by being kind, helpful and assuring. All three must be present to turn things around.

Kindness and business don't always go together. Entrepreneur Gary Vaynerchuk once said, 'You can be kind and still stand up for yourself and crush it in business.'[55] Sometimes people feel that kindness is a weakness and can be taken advantage of. While this may be so, the benefits of kindness far outweigh the negatives. For example, during the unprecedented heatwave across the UK in summer 2022, Showcase Cinemas offered free movie tickets to vulnerable 'redheads'.[56] This move demonstrates real kindness to their customers given the situation, and while other customers may be annoyed that they weren't included in the offer, the intent behind it demonstrated more kindness than excluding groups of people. There's a famous quote by an unknown author which says, 'In a world where you can be anything, be kind.'

Many people are kind and pleasant, but not helpful and assuring. Kindness alone doesn't equal exceptional service.

I once went to a printing shop to get something (you guessed it) printed. It turned out the format I wanted it printed in couldn't be done in that store. There was a lady behind the counter who was pleasant and said, 'I'm sorry, we can't print that for you here, I'm afraid.' That was all.

Even if your product or service can't help a customer, there is no reason why you cannot look for other ways to be helpful. In this situation, she could have suggested a competitor, tried to navigate around the situation or given me something to make me leave thinking she was not only kind but helpful as well. An apology simply does not replace effort to help someone and is used to hide behind when service providers know they are not delivering. To quote comedian Bill Burr, 'Nobody can help, but everybody understands'.[57]

The one thing I have learned while running my own business is that I hate letting people down. It doesn't mean I can do everything myself though, and when I can't, I look for other ways to be helpful to the customer, which doesn't let them down. To quote Hippocrates, 'Make a habit of two things – to help, or at least, to do no harm.'[58]

Sometimes in being kind to someone we have to tell them the truth. To not use discretion for whatever reason may be kind to the customer in the long run. Or it may be kind to other customers that the rule protects. A parking officer that fines someone for parking over an hour in a ten-minute zone outside a takeaway café is being kind to the café owner by issuing a fine, and also being kind to the countless customers who would want to park there in the future. By allowing someone to park longer means the business could lose customers because there's never parking for them to get their coffees.

Politeness is also another word that is used interchangeably with being pleasant and kind. Some service givers are so polite they stay silent in an effort to not offend or upset.

Sometimes saying or doing something is right, and it's what the customer needs to hear.

We've all been in the situation when we give our order to a waiter at a restaurant. Sometimes they don't write it down and you wonder whether they will remember or not. On this occasion, your order is more complex, but the waiter doesn't write it down. While you're waiting for your meal you ponder on whether the waiter will remember everything. Sure enough the waiter returns with your meal, and, as you suspected, it's not exactly what you ordered. (It is completely awesome when a waiter remembers a long and complex order, but this is seen to be more theatrical rather than service focused.)

Our role in service is to be completely assuring to our customers. Think about a simple acknowledgement. It can be assuring to a customer when they know you've seen them. Even if you know they are waiting, explicitly giving an acknowledgement is more about the customer's reassurance than your own.

Much of this book has focused on service being outward-facing toward a customer, but this can also be inward from a customer to an organisation. During the Covid-19 pandemic, restaurants faced significant capacity restrictions and found that no-shows to reservation bookings could mean up to 50% of restaurant capacity not turning up.

I'm not one to no-show to my restaurant bookings, but I can see the circumstances in which people would, perhaps thinking the slots would be filled with walk-ins. Understanding how a no-show could impact a restaurant also illustrates how customers should think in kindness to businesses. This is why many restaurants are now including booking fees to hold a reservation.

I love Adam Grant's view on kindness: 'You reciprocate a favor by paying it back. You honor an act of kindness by paying it forward.'[59] When we are kind to others, it will create a domino effect of kindness.

The goal of all the three character traits – giving, discretion and effort – is to never lose a customer due to a product or service failure. Your staff need to be able to come from a place of giving, use discretion for the sake of the relationship and apply effort because they want to demonstrate to the customer how determined they are to make it right.

Doing whatever it takes to keep your customers also has financial metrics attached to it. Research by management consultancy Bain and Company in the financial services industry found that a 5% increase in customer retention produced more than a 25% increase in profit.[60] Increased purchases, lower operating costs and increased price premiums create this profit formula, but it's the service that makes it possible. In fact, a survey by Walker found that 86% of customers would pay a higher price if it meant they would receive a superior level of service.[61]

The Jumeirah Group hotel chain puts all three of these into action with its 'Stay Different' philosophy. One of its core promises is, 'Our first response to a guest will never be no.' When you think about hotel guests, it's the intention of the hotel to make them feel at home (although that doesn't mean they don't need to wear bathers in the pool), therefore, the staff may have to give more, use discretion and apply extra effort. This philosophy and culture is why the Jumeirah Group stands out from the rest.[62] In *The New Gold Standard*, Joseph Michelli talks about globally famous and real-life examples of the 'legendary customer service' from The Ritz-Carlton hotel chain.[63]

As I conclude this chapter, it is fair to say that many of the assertions about character are rather generous or forgiving to many people (the word is magnanimous). It may well be true that there are many not so good people in the world but even if we think they are unlikely to work in your organisation, they may well come through the doors. This presents a huge challenge for leaders, but I encourage you to feel into this process of character. Have an open mind and the willingness to use these character traits to learn more about the people who are serving others.

In the third part of the book, I will introduce specific actions that you as a leader can take to ensure you are attracting the right people to your organisation if your current team is struggling with these character traits.

7
Attitude

Attitudes overcome obstacles

We spent the last chapter talking about character, and it is character that drives our attitudes, something we hold internally. They are generally the fixed ways we think and feel about something. For example, when you think about anything that's topical in the world today, things such as weather, politics, religion or the latest television show, it is likely we will have a particular attitude toward it.

While attitudes are enduring, they can also change. It's easier to change one's attitude than changing one's character, but it will take work. Before we look at attitudes to service within the culture of your organisation, let's spend a moment running through how attitudes are formed and how they can be changed.

If we think about anything that happens in our lives, our experiences both good and bad have a role to play in forming attitudes. Bad experiences can make us feel strongly against something. Social or societal norms also play a role in forming and changing attitudes – as society changes, it can help force people to shift their attitudes due to the tension that forms between where one person is and where society is. For example, during the Covid-19 pandemic, mask wearing became the norm. Those who didn't wear masks became the minority and whenever there was any uncertaintly about wearing one or not, you would just have to look at what everyone else was doing for your answer. Most leaders are convinced that there is a societal shift happening when it comes to customer service, but there is a lag between the changing customer expectations and the wider workforce in realising and fully accepting this change.

These two influences (life experiences and societal changes) are not the only influences that can change attitude. There are two other smaller and direct ways leaders can use. The smaller influences on attitude are where the magic lies in relation to your organisation and building a service culture. Our learning is something that changes attitudes. It started with school, but as adults and in the workplace, learning programs are usually designed to bring about changes in attitudes.

We can't spend our entire lives in the classroom, so the final, more micro, influence of attitude change is by observation, which occurs when we have role models and leaders to gently but successfully help change an attitude. The challenge with observation is that people in the workplace who don't do the right things can get in the minds of impressionable people and slowly make their attitudes change for the worse. This is why it is important to have suitable role models.

One of our biggest challenges is that being of service to one another is not taught in schools. People have to wait for their first job to learn what it means to serve, and the learning isn't always effective. If your workplace has one or two people who contribute to a toxic culture – who gossip, can't tolerate customers and aren't genuinely interested in people – it's likely these people will begin to shift the attitudes of younger or newer impressionable people who join your organisation. As a leader you need to tighten down on any tolerance there currently is for disruptive employees as they can destroy the efforts you're about to make.

The reason why attitudes are important is because it's attitude that leads to behaviour. If we have the wrong attitude, we will likely exhibit the wrong behaviours, which leads to the customer experiencing poor service. Think about a time when someone you know or care about has a change in attitude toward you. It's not necessarily what they specifically do, but you can always tell that something isn't right.

Regardless of whether your staff behave or deliver service the way you expect, you must not overlook their attitudes, as customers can see past the functional or technical behaviours your staff perform and will be able to see the attitudes they bring to it. For example, you can tell when someone does something reluctantly. People can also pretend or give the illusion they have the right attitude about something, but it's evident in their behaviour that they were only paying lip service to you and the rest of your team. Either way you look at it, attitude is noticeable and needs to be focused on.

Every business regardless of size will have obstacles and challenges. While these challenges can sometimes be predicted, it would be unfair to expect that we can create an environment where your business is never affected by things outside of your control. The power lies in how these obstacles are dealt with. The attitudes I will discuss have been reverse engineered from these common obstacles.

Service is non-negotiable, but as things crop up, the wrong attitude leads to excuses which push service down the list of priorities. We need to equip our workforce with the attitudes that are required to overcome the common and predictable obstacles that are thrown their way and keep service at the front of their minds.

A way to think of this chapter is that service itself isn't an attitude, but there can be attitudes of service. Equally, service shouldn't be a company value (as it should be a given), but there can be values of service. These will be introduced in the next section.

QUESTIONS TO CONSIDER

- What are your attitudes around customer service and how do you deal with problems in the workplace?
- What common issues do you experience in the workplace that get in the way of customer service?

Create service role models

Close your eyes for a moment and visualise what a customer service role model would look like in your organisation? Think about a person that completely epitomises what it means to be of service. Create an image of what this person looks like, sounds like and what they are specifically doing in the moment. Now that you've thought of this person, is there someone like that in your organisation? Is this person a role model to everyone else? While you should be one of the service role models, there is a misconception that there should only be one or two of them. Your goal should be to create an entire organisation of service role models.

Years ago, I read an interesting article about the most frustrating thing people endure in their jobs. It ranked these in order from biggest to smallest. The list was huge and included people leaving dirty dishes in the lunchroom sink and people eating tinned tuna in the lunchroom as everyone hated the smell. What could be worse than leaving a dirty plate of your tuna in the sink for someone else to clean up? The number one frustration was the organisational leader's tolerance of other employees who didn't pull their weight. Think about your frustrations earlier in your career – was this one of them?

While that article is old, there is more recent research that illustrates the same problem. A 2019 study by the Australian Human Resources Institute (AHRI) found that almost 40% of respondents from companies with more than 5,000 staff found their organisation did not have tolerance toward employees who put their own successes ahead of customers and share-holders.[64] That means over 60% tolerated this.

The quickest way to build a culture of service in your organisation is to fill it with service role models that others can observe and aspire to be like. Imagine you have an organisation full of customer service role models, and someone new joins the business. Imagine this person might have slipped through the recruitment process and isn't the best cultural fit. As this person starts work, they will be faced with a decision. They arrived with their own experiences and views on societal pressures. They come through your onboarding process and join the workplace with all your other role models. They have a choice. Change attitude and conform (to the microsociety created in your organisation), or ignore their observations and the training and self-select out.

Your goal is to create the right culture when new people join the business, and if this is so powerful that the wrong person chooses to self-select out, ultimately your business will continue to exhibit this culture. If this employee was to stay, and their performance and attitudes tolerated, you would be stereotypically conforming to be an organisation that tolerates poor performance. The strong cultures out there are the ones that have the right attitudes and don't tolerate the wrong ones. As author Perry Belcher reportedly said, 'Nothing will kill a great employee faster than watching you tolerate a bad one.'

With the case for a role model established, if the people in your organisation aren't role models, then what are they? If you think of your organisation as a team sport and your people as the players, there are a number of 'positions' that can be formed. These positions are shown in the following 'attitudes' model.

OBSTACLES		ATTITUDES
NO CHANGE →	ROLE MODELS ←	BE UNIQUE
NO CLARITY →	TEAM PLAYERS ←	BE OPTIMISTIC
NO RESOURCES →	MEMBERS ←	BE INNOVATIVE
NO CREDIBILITY →	NOVICES ←	BE ENERGETIC
NO ALIGNMENT →	OPPONENTS	← BE ACCOUNTABLE

ADOPTION

Attitudes Model

Working from most undesired to desired, the first position is known as the 'opponent'. While this person is still on your team, they are kicking goals for the competition. They are directly going against the things you are trying to create.

The next position is the 'novice' or 'rookie'. Usually labelled as the new recruit or someone playing their first season of the game, this person could also be someone who's been with you for a while yet are still operating at this level.

The middle position is known as the 'member'. These are the ones that blend in among the many, do their jobs and coast along. You couldn't survive without them, but they're not doing much to add considerable value.

The second-best position is the 'team players'. They are just that. There is long-term potential for them, they're an asset for your team and while they have more to learn, in time they can be a role model.

Finally, there is the 'role model' or 'role models'. These are the people that epitomise what it means to be of service to others. If your organisation could be full of these people, you would be ecstatic. They can lead and be an inspiration for others to follow.

Generally speaking, the people in your organisation will distribute themselves according to these positions. Using the five headings and descriptions, take a moment to categorise your people under those headings from a service perspective.

Earlier in this chapter we discussed how the right attitude will overcome the known obstacles that can appear in your organisation. We discussed that there is no way to completely prevent obstacles and challenges from coming your way. If we reverse engineer the obstacle and find the right attitude to overcome this, your people can push through adversity while maintaining focus on their customers.

The list of obstacles that exist in business is huge. However, there are five common ones that directly affect attitudes and service. The remainder of this chapter will explore each of the obstacles and introduce the attitude needed to overcome it. The obstacles can be ranked from most impactful to less impactful, but the attitudes must feed into one another. Your staff members must have all five attitudes if they are to be a service role model in your organisation. The obstacles and corresponding attitudes are also shown in the model.

Be accountable

The biggest obstacle to creating a culture of service is a lack of alignment in the organisation. By alignment I'm talking about 'what is preached isn't necessarily practised'.

Leaders can do a good job of making big declarations – telling everyone that things are changing, highlighting that customer service is important, saying all the right things and meaning it – until something gets in the way to distract them. When this happens, the people within the organisation say things like: 'So then, what's the point?' 'Why should I bother?' 'Ah yeah, do as I say, not as I do.'

This can also happen at a microlevel. One department is doing all the right things and pulling their weight, but the other departments or colleagues in their department start to lose sight of customer service. Therefore, people completely give up. This is dangerous as once someone gives up or loses their drive to be of service, they can quickly become opponents and, in turn, create other opponents within the team.

While the goal is to ensure things operate in alignment, if it's out of alignment even for a split second, your people need to be equipped with the attitude to overcome any distraction away from customers.

The first attitude is accountability. In being accountable, your people can stay focused on their service, even when faced with conflicting priorities and especially if other people don't perform in the same way. What's great about accountability is that people focus more on themselves and the role they play, which protects them from entering into a culture of blame. Once people start blaming others, it's hard for them to see it as a problem. They feel good because the pressure is seemingly shifted off them and on to someone else.

It doesn't escape the problem, but it gives the illusion the problem is no longer there.

The biggest challenge is being the only person who is accountable when everyone around you isn't. In the previous chapter we explored discretion, which is directly relatable here. If no one in the organisation uses their discretion, then it's really difficult to be the only one who does.

As Mahatma Gandhi reportedly said, 'If we could change ourselves, the tendencies in the world would also change. As a man changes his own nature, so does the attitude of the world change towards him.' The more people that are accountable, the more likely it is that those tempted to become opponents will stop and be accountable themselves. This means there are fewer people that you as a leader need to work on to bring back into alignment.

There's an old saying that the windscreen of a car is the biggest, the rear-view mirror is the smallest and the side mirrors are big enough to check but only from time to time. It implies the main focus should be on where you're driving, with less focus on what's happening on the side and behind. The same is true for service. It's not helpful to keep looking at what other people are doing around you if it will make you lose sight of how you are serving your customers.

QUESTIONS TO CONSIDER

- Can my team can stay service focused even when faced with conflicting priorities?
- Can my team can stay service focused even when other people don't pull their weight?

Be energetic

In the 1999 movie *Office Space*, uninspiring manager Bill Lumbergh (played by Gary Cole) announces at a staff meeting that 'next Friday is Hawaiian shirt day' as a fun engagement idea for his staff. The camera pans to the workforce standing up and staring with no emotion, completely uninspired about the prospect of dressing up at work. It's safe to say that Bill Lumbergh has lost credibility with his staff.

A leader must be inspiring and relentless with their messaging in general, but specifically service messaging (something we will explore in Chapter 12). If a leader has lost credibility among the workforce, they will struggle to be motivating. A CEO should be known as the 'chief energy officer' as it's their role to bring energy to everyone in the organisation around customer service.

The messaging itself must also be well thought through. Anyone can say that service is the number one priority and market to customers that a business is service driven. While this seems like something that will engage a workforce, it's usually where the disconnect forms. If you're not clear, your staff won't know what's expected of them, and so they act like a rookie. This lack of energy within the organisation means as a leader you are constantly forced to remind people that service is important.

The attitude needed here is one of energy. If people have an energetic approach to serving others, they won't need to rely on messaging (both internal and external) to remind them. Sure, you still need to be inspiring and motivating, but if people have already adopted an energetic attitude about serving others, they will be meeting you halfway.

In the last chapter we talked about how effort is something that goes across both business and life. An energetic attitude, on the other hand, is something that can be switched on and off. The staff at Disneyland are referred to as cast members and whenever they walk into a customer-facing area they are going 'on stage' and in the lunchroom they are 'backstage'. As a leader your aim should be to make sure people are switched on whenever they are in front of their customers.

The last chapter also explored applying effort as a way to give others confidence, instead of just being confident. The energetic approach to messaging works the same way. Being 'on stage' in front of your staff is one way to create confidence in them. Energy isn't the only ingredient. Your messages need to be delivered with conviction and in a congruent way. The formula is Conviction + Congruency = Confidence in the other person.

QUESTIONS TO CONSIDER

- Are my people enthusiastic about serving others?
- Do I need to constantly remind my staff that service is important?

Be innovative

This is my favourite obstacle. Not that I should have a favourite, but it's the one that is probably the most common yet easiest and most fun to fix.

A few years ago, I was delivering a program for a group of legal assistants who worked in a call centre at a family law firm. As we were talking about customer service, a few of the staff told me they could only provide the level of service we were discussing if they had more staff, as the workload was unmanageable as it was.

Without knowing how the conversation would flow, I asked the following questions, and these were their answers.

I asked, 'What is the busiest day and time of the week for you?'

They responded, 'Monday morning at 9am.' (Weekends can be a prime time for family arguments, and they expected a higher volume of calls every Monday morning.)

I then asked, 'When do you have your staff meetings?'

They responded, 'Monday morning at 9am.'

So, I asked, 'When is the quietest day and time of the week?'

They responded, 'Tuesday afternoons.'

I suggested, 'Is there any reason you couldn't move your Monday morning meeting to Tuesday afternoon?'

To which one person quickly said, 'No way. We've been having Monday morning meetings for over ten years, and they are essential to start the week off on the right foot.'

My final question was, 'What happens in the Monday morning meeting anyway?'

A different person responded by saying, 'The meeting usually starts late by the time everyone has grabbed a coffee and taken their seats. We usually talk about who got voted off the reality TV show last night before making our way through the reports from last week. We generally wrap up the meeting by 10.30am because it's morning teatime.'

The group may well have been short staffed, but I didn't buy for one second that staffing was the only thing getting in the way of the ability to serve customers; in fact, it just seemed to be an excuse. Being short staffed is often an excuse, and while in terms of total capacity it may be true, organisations such as hotels continue to sell rooms to customers knowing they don't have the staff to serve them effectively. Sometimes it would be wiser to reduce capacity when staffing levels are low, than keep it high and not serve them effectively.

Innovation is another buzzword right now, but it's a useful one. If your team has an innovative attitude to their work and customer service, they will be able to identify things that are getting in the way of serving their customers. They will be able to reprioritise tasks in favour of the ones that have a direct impact to the customer or think of doing the same things in different ways to achieve a better result. Innovation in this sense is not about coming up with new ideas (more on that later in the book), but rather recognising and making changes in established processes or methods to improve customer service.

The obstacle in this case is that over time our workloads increase with tasks that seem important in the moment, and they continue to build on top of each other. These may come in the form of reporting. If a new report was added each year for someone to complete and none get taken away, it would significantly eat into the service time expected.

While I'm not saying reports and data aren't useful, when people have an innovative attitude, they are able to question their relevance. I once worked for a company where leaders were expected to complete their weekly report by midweek to give the other leaders a chance to read them before discussing the same reports at the weekly meeting. It turned out that not only was writing the reports taking valuable time, but nobody read them. Other organisations have found that the cost of lost time in producing reports could be put into hiring a data analyst whose sole job would be to compile and review data. Management consultant Peter Drucker is widely attributed to have said, 'There's nothing so useless as doing efficiently that which should not be done at all.'

Businesses must figure out how to meet their profit targets while also meeting their customers' expectations. Kenneth B Elliott reputedly said, 'Customers are dependent on us, were not dependent on them. They are not an interruption to our work, they are the purpose of it. They are not outsiders, they're part of it. We're not doing them a favour; they are doing us a favour by giving us the opportunity to do so.'

If you can make savings on labour through these efficiencies, consider how you could use these savings to invest in service for the organisation. This section is not about overstaffing. This is about having an attitude to be innovative and look at how to serve customers better when inundated with the things that don't matter. Many businesses are used to this already.

Coming out of the Covid-19 pandemic, leaders were required to navigate around government mandates to do business as usual. This required more effort to put safeguards and other measures in place for the same result, if not less. This means that leaders must be service minded when faced with regulatory disruptions and look for innovative ways to deliver service to customers under the difficult circumstances. Think about some of the other disruptions that could occur – it may not be a pandemic, but it's the pandemic that's given businesses good experience in this area.

Even if staff members are completely focused on their customers in frontline service roles and not distracted by non-customer-facing tasks, it is important to consider how they are providing customer service instead of assuming that there are not enough staff. For example, in 2018, Centrelink (a social security division of the Australian Government) increased their call centres by 1,000 employees as they were grappling to deal with an increase of 26 million calls year-on-year to a total of 55 million calls from customers.[65] While this figure is huge, and increasing staffing would be one possible solution, businesses should review whether there are any roadblocks during the calls that are not being dealt with instead of looking at the calls that remain unanswered.

For example, some staff might be stuck on dealing with difficult customers, going around in circles, having to escalate issues or repeat issues that weren't properly documented before. If the business could investigate and remove these roadblocks, the call times may decrease. This would offer a better experience for customers on a call and free up the operator to take the next call quicker, reducing call durations and wait times.

When people use lack of time and resources as an excuse, their attitude at work is that of a 'member'. Staff will say things like, 'It is what it is, I'll get to it when I can' or 'If only there were three of me', and while this attitude and approach is not as destructive as the one of an opponent, it will act as a barrier to building a culture of service. When organisations can't get past this barrier, things stagnate.

QUESTIONS TO CONSIDER

- Can my team identify things that get in the way of serving customers?
- Are my team are able to prioritise tasks that have a direct impact on the customer?

Be optimistic

We've reached your 'team players'. Let's do a quick recap. A team player is accountable for playing their part. They are energetic and innovative in everything they do – a perfect combination so far.

What stops a team player from becoming a role model is the fatigue associated with building a service culture. In Chapter 14, I will talk about some of the metrics that can signify whether you're making progress. Sometimes we don't get the immediate feedback that our efforts are working. Being an organisation that's renowned for a service culture is great and inspiring, but it's a long road ahead.

Misadvice tells people on these sorts of journeys to 'be positive' which isn't useful as it's hard to stay positive. While a team player is on board with your service efforts, and is hoping for everything to fall into place, they can lack the faith required.

In any form of cultural change, the past will be lurking in the background. The grievances that exist about the old days haven't gone away, and the future looks no better as it's filled with unease, anxiety, stress, tension, worry and fear about what's around the corner.

A team player is on board with things, but they can't see into the long term as you can because, to them, things are still unclear. The attitude required when clarity is missing is optimism. If we can get our staff to see the long-term nature of this sort of work, the value they provide and the difference they are making to others, they will be able to push through these challenging times with an optimistic attitude. It's great to be positive and have hope, but it's even more important to have faith and optimism.

QUESTIONS TO CONSIDER

- Does my team see customer service as a long-term commitment?
- Can my team see the value and difference their service makes to others?

Be unique

Role models serve every customer differently. If you observed them, they would be winning with all of them. They stand out because they are in tune to both the needs and wants of their customers and can adapt accordingly. They are also able to express themselves naturally to customers. We obviously want lots of role models, but the point here is that every role model will appear unique. They serve customers in 'their way' and are not a carbon copy of everyone else. Regardless of what changes, or what product knowledge they're missing, they will find a way to get through it.

Someone who is a role model is connected to their customers. This would apply to you as a leader too. Anecdotal reports said that Walt Disney spent a lot of time inside the theme park and his studios – not behind his desk. Richard Branson is also famously known for not having a desk and never working in an office.[66] A leader should in a calendar year spend the equivalent of one week working on the frontline serving customers – this is approximately one day every 2.5 months.

In the previous chapter, I talked about discretion and making decisions without deferring to a manager. There may be an exception to the rule, and one of the biggest frustrations between staff members and customers alike is when the managers are hard to reach. By being connected to customers on the frontline, you are visibly present and staff members can reach you in the circumstances when they absolutely need to.

QUESTIONS TO CONSIDER

- Are my team in tune with their customers and adapting to their changing needs and wants?
- Can my team figure out how to deal with a variety of customer situations on their own?
- Do I have a role model for these attitudes in my team?

A role model not only has a unique attitude; they also have all the attitudes we've discussed combined and are able to overcome misalignment by being accountable for themselves. When credibility is lacking, they show energy. When time and resources appear to constrain them, they think innovatively. They're optimistic about the future even though the future may not be clear. Finally, they overcome change by looking at each customer and each situation uniquely.

You can't have a service culture without these attitudes: A for accountability, E for energetic, I for innovative, O for optimistic and U for unique. A-E-I-O-U.

8
Behaviour

Realistic and observable ways to serve

Character drives attitude, and attitude drives behaviour. We've officially crossed the line between what our staff hold internally to them, to what they display externally.

Behaviour is the way a person acts or conducts themselves. While your business is a team of individuals, it's possible to create the same behaviours across the entire workforce if you've brought out the right character and attitudes in each person. Behaviours will occur naturally with or without intervention. Exceptional customer service requires a specific set of behaviours that you, as a leader, must actively try to instil across the team.

Coming up with behaviours for your organisation initially seems to be one of the easiest tasks. Many jump straight to this step and create the behaviours, but they don't work in the long run. The problem with designing behaviours is that they must work across all situations and all departments. There are a range of desired behaviours we associate with exceptional service, but, in practice, as situations change, the behaviours are not always appropriate.

One of the most common behaviours organisations attempt to instil is to 'always smile'. It seems like good advice but there are a couple of problems with this. When you're in a serious mood and someone tells you to smile, how does it make you feel? It might work, but it can also have the opposite effect. It can feel forced.

As a global Coca-Cola campaign once said, 'Happiness starts with a smile.'[67] It showed an actor in disguise boarding a train on the Antwerp Metro in Belgium laughing at something he was watching on his tablet. There were hidden cameras secretly filming and, before long, the entire carriage was in stitches of laughter. A smile and a laugh are definitely contagious, but this doesn't mean it should be a forced behaviour.

A happy person should smile freely. If you must give your staff instructions to smile, it could indicate that they are not happy to begin with. Have you checked? Or someone smiling at us can make things worse. If you're in a serious moment talking to someone or making a complaint, the smile on the other person's face can make you want to scream.

There is one small exception to the rule – something which I have observed during organisational responses to the Covid-19 pandemic. Staff members who wore masks or who were only communicating over the phone were forgetting to smile. If we smile behind our face masks, it shows in our eyes. If we smile while on the telephone, you can hear it in our voice. If we smile when we're walking, we may not look like we're on a serious mission. There is a good reason to smile, but it's not something we should impose as standard behaviour.

Treat people like guests in your home

There are different words used for the term 'customers'. Some industries use customers, health funds use the word members, hospitals use the word patients, airlines use the word passengers, universities use students, tourism attractions use visitors, and hotels use the word guests. I prefer not to entertain the many debates that exist between them. While there are subtle nuances, it's not useful or productive to be petty over them.

What you call your customer is one thing, but how you treat them is another. Of the words above, the one that I find most useful when it comes to how we treat other people is the word 'guest'. In Chapter 6, we talked about the Jumeirah Group and how they want to make their guests feel at home. It's easy for hotels to do this, but rather than just looking at them for inspiration, take a look at what you do at home. Making visitors feel at home is something we do without even thinking about it.

Imagine you are hosting a party at your house. Maybe you're someone that handwrites every single invitation or creates an event on social media and sends a bulk invite. Perhaps you give a formal starting time, or you might tell people to come whenever. It might be that you open the side gate so people can enter as they please or make them ring the front doorbell. You could ask everyone to bring a plate or

149

tell them not to bring a thing. With all these options, there's one thing that unites a good host – you want your guests to enjoy themselves.

I remember as a kid when someone visited. Our house wasn't messy, but there was extra effort put in for our guests. I remember my mum bringing out the special tablecloth that was only used when people came over. Many of the things we do personally can be transitioned into our workplace service. If we can connect people to what they already do, it will be far easier to bring these out in your organisation.

American fast-food chain Chick-fil-A was recognised as the politest chain in the restaurant business. In a survey which included nearly 2,000 visits to fifteen different fast-food chains, in 95.2% of drive-thru encounters their employees said 'thank you'. By way of comparison, Kentucky Fried Chicken (KFC) had a 'thank you' rate of 84.9%, and McDonald's rate was 78.4%, putting it in fourteenth place out of the fifteen.[68] It goes to show that the basics we're taught in childhood are not necessarily translating to interactions with our customers. A rate of 95.2% is great, but would that figure be acceptable to you?

If we can reverse engineer how you want people to feel in your house and translate this into the workplace, we can come up with the realistic, actionable and observable behaviours which can make this happen.

Here are nine common steps taken when a guest arrives at your home:

1. You greet them – you want to make them feel that they **belong**.

2. You invite them in and tell them to relax – you want them to feel **comfortable**.

3. You offer them a drink or something to eat – you want to show them you're **prepared**.

4. You'll have a conversation with them and ask them questions – you want to be an **approachable** host.

5. As time passes, you check and ask if you can get them another drink or something to eat – you want to make the experience **effortless** for them.

6. You keep them **interested** – this might be by playing the music they like or thinking of something to do that will make them want to stay.

7. As the visit draws to a close, you tell them 'we should do this again' because you want them to **return**.

8. As they leave, you look at them and show you are **grateful** by saying 'thanks for coming'.

9. As they leave, you'll bid them farewell in a **genuine** manner – you might wait at the front door until they leave or stand on the driveway waving them off.

These behaviours are shown in the following model and typically follow the cycle of an interaction from start to finish.

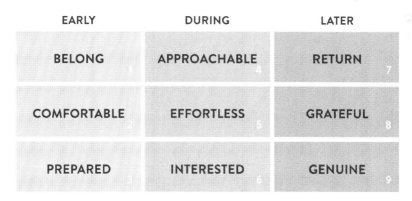

Behaviours Model

Why can't we come up with specific behaviours that contribute to these outcomes in the workplace? The challenge is that for them to work, they must be specific to your organisation. You can't just copy and paste them from this book and expect them to work. For the remainder of this chapter, I will share examples of how behaviours could be created for each of these nine categories.

Signature service standards – nine behaviours

When I was ten years old, I attended a funeral for the first time. In the cortege of vehicles, I sat directly behind the driver of the last car. It was here that I noticed something that fascinated me. The driver of the vehicle wouldn't get in until all the drivers of all the other vehicles and hearse in front of them were in position. The driver of the first vehicle led the rest in getting into their cars at exactly the same time. This showed reverence, professionalism and attention to detail – something you would expect from a funeral director. This action is also a signature service standard, something that is always done, that is just part of the way they do things.

This chapter is not just about helping you come up with service behaviours, but rather coming up with signature service standards that will be the specific way your organisation does things. This section will work through the nine categories shown in the model, looking at the behaviours appropriate for each one. Workshop these with specific departments to ensure the strategies you adopt are relevant for them. Note the examples can be translated to many other areas of your business, not just front-facing roles.

Remember the phrase 'more good is good, less bad is better'? Keep these words in mind as we discover our behaviours.

To remove the 'less bad' that drags performance down, it's useful to assess what you are doing that repels or puts customers off. Then come up with two lists: first, a list of behaviours you want to see, and, second, a list of behaviours you don't want to see.

Belong

It's important to consider whether customers truly feel they belong in your organisation. This could be achieved by looking up at them (if sitting down when they approach you), greeting them as soon as they approach you or join the queue, or giving them your undivided attention (by stopping what you are doing while interacting with them). Do you see how all of these are specific enough that you could easily do them with every customer as well as observe them from a leadership perspective?

While staff members assumingly don't want customers to feel that they don't belong, there are several behaviours that could unintentionally do what you're trying to avoid. Write these behaviours down in the list of what you don't want to see. They could include, but are not limited to, being engrossed in tasks and multitasking, avoiding customers and turning their backs to counters for long periods of time.

Comfortable

Creating an environment where customers feel comfortable is achieved by helping them relax or feel at ease. It's the little things in service that make the difference. Your staff could adopt a no rushing or running policy. They could tell customers to take their time or ask them additional questions to make the service process feel less robotic or rushed. They could ditch jargon and listen more carefully to requests. A customer should never feel like an inconvenience.

To unintentionally make a customer wait awkwardly isn't making them feel comfortable. Using jargon or finishing their sentences should also be put on the not to do list. When these things happen, your customers will shy away from asking you further questions. Have you ever not asked a question because you thought the person serving you didn't want to help you and that you were an inconvenience for them? Cleaning or packing away around a customer can also make them feel uncomfortable.

Prepared

It's surprising how often staff members reveal to a customer that they've been caught off guard or are completely unprepared for what they need. When this happens, it is evident that their focus is moment to moment and they are not thinking ahead.

Examples of this behaviour include checking in with a customer if you notice their body language says they are confused or thinking ahead to what they might need further down the track. It's common for staff to think of their own product and service, but not how that product fits into everything else the customer might want to achieve. If I engaged an architect to design a house for me, I would expect them to be able to recommend a builder once they'd finished drawing it.

It's the little behaviours that show you are unprepared such as not having a pen or paper ready, or not having the right computer program or screen open before you serve a customer. These are the things you want to see less of.

Approachable

Customers shouldn't have to approach your staff, if your staff can beat them to it. Saying 'hi' to customers as you pass them is way to show you are approachable and they may ask you a question or for some assistance. There is nothing worse than a staff member who avoids eye contact with a customer. When I first started working in retail there was that cringeworthy two-metre rule where you had to walk up to everyone within two-metres and acknowledge them. I don't think anyone ever did it and things have moved on from then. However, walking past a customer and noticing them (even without a formal acknowledgement) may result in the customer getting your attention to ask a question that they otherwise wouldn't have.

If staff members are waiting for a customer, their body language is important. Having open body language makes staff members look approachable as opposed to standing with their arms folded, which would put anyone off.

Effortless

Out of all the behaviours, this one is the most important because it's often the most overlooked. Most people don't have a problem with making things effortless for your customers, as long as they don't have to work harder. There should be a mantra in your organisation to make things effortless – even if you have to work harder. Any behaviour that achieves this is worth noting, whether it be helping someone complete a form, using Google to find an answer or a place that stocks what they are looking for, putting a lid on their coffee, or taking them to an item instead of pointing them in the right direction. There is a local coffee shop near me that also keeps the 'coffee stamp loyalty card' indexed by names at the counter, so the customer doesn't need to remember to bring it with them each time.

There are some pitfalls you should be aware of though. If a staff member isn't service minded, they will likely push effort or onus back on to the customer. If you've ever heard a staff member tell a customer 'please call back' if someone isn't available (instead of taking a message and getting the other person to call them back) or 'follow up with me next week to check on progress' (rather than making a note to keep the customer informed on progress), they are not making things effortless for customers.

In the previous chapter, we talked about how admin tasks seem to be growing your to-do list. The same thing is subtly happening with customers. If you think about retail, a customer used to be able to make a purchase easily then leave. Now, there is a push to make a donation, sign-up to a program, answer a survey question or apply for a card. Giving customers lots of things to do adds time and effort to their shopping experience, and you could be putting them off.

As the saying goes, 'The only effort should be in the maintenance of effortlessness.' If a staff member is not service minded, they will likely think of effortlessness as being a 'slave' to a customer. If this is still happening, something in the attitude or character steps are missing.

Interested

Keeping a customer interested is a difficult task, but, as discussed in Chapter 4, when we link needs versus wants with Maslow's hierarchy of needs, our customers want to be connected to something bigger. This isn't about boring customers or telling them the pros and cons of working in your business. It's about getting your staff to share something 'interesting' about the backstory, the environmental impact, commitment to charities or the higher purpose of what's being achieved. Do this and they will captivate the customers more easily.

When my wife and I were engaged to be married, we met a couple of photographers to chat about using their services for our wedding. One of the photographers sat down, opened her notebook and started asking questions about the wedding date and location. In contrast, the other wedding photographer sat down and left her notebook closed. She asked us how long we had been together, where we met and how the proposal was made. Neither was rude, but the second photographer (which we ended up using) demonstrated interest in us.

Employee name badges at the Westin Hotel in Bali also have a special interest written on them. It might be sport, travel or music. It's the most inviting things that generate conversations with customers.

Want to return

This is a bonus category. Anything extra that your staff can 'do' for the customer could trigger them to want to return. For instance, if a customer asks for something that's out of stock, doing the extra research to find out when the delivery is due could persuade them to come back.

If you make your customers feel like a burden, don't resolve their issue or miss promised deadlines, they will go elsewhere next time. Look for the golden nuggets your staff can carry out easily or ask them what they've tried before that's resulted in a positive outcome for the customer. They can share these examples with other staff members.

Grateful

Gratitude is where those 'thank yous' we discussed earlier come into play. Use them as much as possible, including saying to a customer 'thank you for waiting' no matter how short the queue. Being grateful, like each behaviour discussed previously, simply makes customers feel good. It's just like when a pedestrian crossing a crosswalk thanks you, the motorist, for stopping. You're obliged to stop, but it still feels nice to receive a wave when someone is grateful. Staff often assume the person knows they are grateful, so they don't demonstrate it, and we don't see as many 'thank yous' as we should.

Sometimes customers will do something nice for staff. They might give positive feedback or pick something up if your staff member drops it. When this happens, no matter how small, your staff should be demonstrating they are grateful.

A quick way to increase gratitude is to observe how often leaders show gratitude to their staff. If they model the desired behaviour, there is a greater chance that staff will display it to their customers.

Genuine

It is much easier to behave in a genuine way if your staff members are 'being' of service versus 'doing' service with their customers. Speaking from the heart, avoiding robotic phrases, remembering someone and their name, and asking each customer if there is anything else they can help with are examples of where staff can be more genuine.

It's common for customers to not even be farewelled. It seems like such a basic thing, but it's worth checking if your staff members are saying goodbye or any other appropriate phrase as the customer is leaving. In the hotel industry, staff members are encouraged to add something to make the farewell feel more genuine. Therefore, at a seaside resort, if a customer is walking out of the hotel with a beach towel, the staff members are trained to say 'Have a nice day at the beach' instead of 'Have a nice day'.

Pausing at the end of an interaction makes the farewell far more genuine than if you were to bid farewell and immediately rush to the next customer in line. If you have to signal a customer to move on by serving the next customer, it hasn't been a genuine farewell (like the post office did to my wife and I in the story from Chapter 1).

Use the behaviours mentioned in these nine categories as a guide. See if they resonate with your team and check they're applicable across all departments. If not, you can keep some and progressively add other ones to the list as they're discovered. At the end of this exercise, you will have more than nine behaviours. In fact, it's quite common to have two to three per category, and that's just for one of your customer-facing departments. When you have your completed list, look at each of your nine categories and identify the core behaviour you want for each. These will become your signature service behaviours.

While it's great to have a list fully completed, it's not something that should be set in stone. Keep the nine categories the same, but feel free to update the behaviours as you see fit. If a behaviour isn't working, remove it.

9
Skill

Service done well

We've reached the final component of what creates a culture of service. Character drives attitude, attitude drives behaviour and behaviours done well are done with skill.

This chapter is about taking it up a level and you may be familiar with some of the themes explored here. This is because in traditional customer service training, they are the skills most focused on. These are commonly referred to as soft skills, and although Simon Sinek refers to them as 'human skills',[69] I think these skills are more difficult to learn than the technical 'hard skills' required of our jobs. As you can see from where it is placed in the book, there's a lot more that comes before it, and a lot more which follows it. Imagine trying to be skilled at something without getting the foundations right first.

It's like learning how to win the Tour de France without knowing how to ride a bike.

Service with skill is service done well. If you are to be renowned for your customer service and culture, this is what that makes it happen. If you've followed the book from the beginning and particularly got the character, attitude and behaviours right, the skill part will be much easier.

While it is true that with the foundations set, anyone can learn to do something with skill, there are many people out there who are naturally talented in this area. If you are lucky enough to have these people in your organisation, this part will happen quicker.

Before we move on, reflect on how well you believe the service to be in your organisation. Remember that skill is what mainly contributes to the lovely things you hear, or will soon be hearing, from your customers. Skill is observable, and there are four things that you can look for that indicate your staff members are serving customers well.

1. They are **deliberate** in their approach to service.

2. They **interact** well with others.

3. They're able to do things that are **memorable**.

4. They can deliver an **experience** your customers want.

These are all shown on the following model and will be explored throughout this chapter.

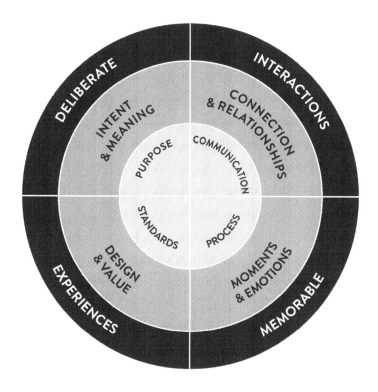

Skill Model

Deliberately make service a reason for coming to work

When you think about the word deliberate, it usually has a negative feel to it. For example, when I watch my son explore boundaries as he learns what he's allowed to touch and what he's not allowed to touch, I love to observe him as he goes near the television. He knows he's not supposed to touch the screen, but he will wander over to it and look at me. I tell him not to touch. He keeps looking for a moment, then deliberately touches it. It's hard to know what's going on in the mind of a toddler, but I could tell he did it deliberately.

To be deliberate means to do something consciously and carefully, with intent. Unlike a child who deliberately pushes boundaries, in service it is something that can be done positively. When someone is serving deliberately, they are consciously putting intent behind everything they do.

As people become more experienced and serve better, their service will be less deliberate and more intuitive. Many see this as a positive, but it's not what we want to achieve. It's like driving a car. If you've had your licence for some time and are confident behind the wheel, it's likely that you don't need to think much about driving as it comes naturally to you. Do you ever arrive at a destination and reflect on how you got there? Or you can't recall seeing a green light or passing through a stop sign on the way? This is because when we drive, we drive intuitively.

There are many things we do every day that we don't think about. Going up and down stairs for instance. Bond University on the Gold Coast in Australia has what they call 'thinking stairs' on their campus. The steps are around 1.5 paces apart so you can't walk them like normal steps. The idea was to slow the pace for students and academics to have time for reflection.

To serve someone intuitively is like being on autopilot. You can form great habits around service, but the act of serving needs to stay deliberate. To serve deliberately requires a high level of motivation. A purpose statement which describes the 'why' we come to work each day is one of the best tools to achieve this.

If you asked your staff why they come to work each day, they would likely say 'to be paid'. Their wages are a tangible item they physically receive as a result of what they do. People need money to pay their bills and to live, but this tangible reason for coming to work is only one-half of it. Without the other half, a staff member will drag themselves to work purely for the money and this will translate into their service. The 'purpose' lies in the intangible reason for coming to work. This reason can't be physically touched or seen but can be felt. You could pose the question – if you didn't need any money, would you still come to work to achieve this purpose?

You may be familiar with Simon Sinek's book *Start With Why*, in which he argues that purpose is all about the 'why'.[70] Many organisations are trying to be more purposeful, but there is an opportunity that exists between your organisation's purpose, and how well this connects to your customers and, in turn, your staff members.

After reading this, you might have a little homework to do, as creating a purpose statement takes time and requires your entire team's inclusion and input to be owned by them. To help create a purpose statement to inspire and motivate your staff to serve others deliberately, I'd like to propose a definition:

Your (P)urpose equals (=) (W)hy your team should do something over (/) (E)verything else. This can be written as $P = W / E$.

Whenever something conflicts with purpose, the purpose should prevail. The Walt Disney Company coined the phrase that sums this up perfectly: 'It's ok to be off-task, if you're on-purpose.'[71]

One of Walt Disney's executives, Van France (who in 1955 was responsible for the first Disneyland training program), proposed the purpose statement (also known as a service vision) to Walt and his brother Roy. He proposed, 'We create happiness for others.' This has evolved subtly over the years, but Van's premise was simple. He said, 'Look, you may park cars, clean up the place, sweep the place, work the graveyard and everything else, but whatever you do is contributing to creating happiness for others.'[72]

Aside from the statement applying to everyone, it's something that should be noticeable daily. It would be hard for the cast members at Disneyland to wake up every morning and jump out of bed to create happiness if they never saw any happy people. When this is in the forefront of minds at every minute of every day, the staff are operating deliberately, with purpose. If a cast member at Disneyland was given two conflicting jobs – hypothetically, one job to file paperwork, but on the way noticed a child in the park who had lost her parents the purpose of creating happiness would override the task of filing paperwork.

What is great about the Disney purpose statement is it is simple, realistic and the results can be observed. I have seen complicated statements that have too many words and are unrealistic, and it's debatable whether they can be achieved or not.

If the purpose statement is to be owned by the entire team, it should be short enough for everyone to remember. As a leader, you should be able to ask any staff member to tell you what it is and get the correct answer every time.

If the statement is important to your team, it must also be important to your customers. Likewise, if it's realistic for your team to deliver, your customers must realistically believe you can deliver it. With Disneyland, 'happiness' is important to customers, and they can be sure they'll get it when they enter the park.

Your current statement might not be that far off. Sometimes half the work is done as it will feature in your marketing or business tag line. For example, food brand MasterFoods have the tag line 'Make dinnertime matter'. This a reason for staff to come to work.

In 1984, Kodak Australia featured a television commercial with the tag line 'Would you trust these moments to anyone but Kodak?' Despite where Kodak is now, if you look deep enough, people working for them were in the business of capturing moments or memories.

When your staff are connected to the purpose and think about it from the moment they get out of bed to the moment they go to bed, you can be assured that they will be approaching their service deliberately.

QUESTIONS TO CONSIDER

- Do you believe your staff think about service consciously?
- Do you know the intangible reason you go to work each day?

Develop connections through customer interactions

There is plenty of evidence that humans love connection, which I agree with. At the same time, more people are becoming disconnected, and younger generations are now connected to technology more than to people. According to research conducted by global accounting firm PricewaterhouseCoopers, 82% of US customers, and 74% of non-US customers, want more human interaction,[73] which is an interesting insight.

For April Fool's Day in 2016, Google released a promotion advertising the new 'Google Cardboard Plastic' which was a set of plastic goggles that allowed people to see 'actual reality'.[74] It was a satire on how everyone is getting into virtual reality and spending more time in the imaginary space than focusing on what's real. We're losing connection with real things in favour of those that are artificial.

When it comes to being of service to others, it is about con-necting and building relationships. Can you say the same for service providers you see regularly – do you feel you have some sort of relationship with them?

Connection is not just being in contact with someone. Nor is it about connecting over the product you're buying. Connection goes beyond this and moves to something greater. For instance, the coffee shop I buy my coffee from purchases beans from South America and roasts them in house. Instead of connecting with me over the coffee I'm buying, the barista and I talk about coffee in general. The more coffee beans I try, the more they remember. This signifies that the relationship is developing.

A connection and relationship are formed when an inter-action takes place, but the term 'interaction' isn't one that's often used in the world of customer service. Instead, we use the word 'transaction'. What do you think the difference is?

A transaction sounds clinical and cold. Like when you make a transaction at an ATM, you're either depositing or withdrawing money. It's something that doesn't require com-munication. Service has been taken over by transactions. There are times when someone who works in 'customer ser-vice' can 'serve' you without communicating at all.

In Chapter 1, I explored how self-service was threaten-ing human connection and how businesses need to evolve to ensure humans can add value to customers. We also need to explore the social and necessary elements of a simple interac-tion in our organisation.

Keeping with the retail example, in 2019, the Jumbo super-market in the Dutch town of Vlijmen introduced a 'Klets Kassa', which can be translated to mean 'Chat Checkout'.[75] The Netherlands (like many other countries) recognises that lone-liness is common, particularly in older people. Introducing the 'Chat Checkout' was not just about taking a stand against self-service but also recognising that customers may be lonely and that their shopping experience is one of the few, if not the only, times they interact with a human.

A slow lane for shoppers seems unthinkable, but when you look at the importance of interaction you can see just how clever this is. It's interesting to compare the 'Chat Checkout' example with instances where organisations are forcing elderly customers to go online or complete self-service. We all know what it feels like when we have to do something for the first time, let alone use technology we've never used before. For some it can be too much to deal with. In 2022, a seventy-eight year-old retiree in Spain managed to get over 312,000 signatures on a viral petition to get banks to have less technology and more human customer care, after he had been told, among other things, to ask his children to do his banking for him.[76]

A two-way interaction doesn't have to be long. Short interactions are also powerful, including simply connecting with a smile. In 2019, a Sudanese man named Hassan Anglo made the news for being the 'happiest trolley collector' in Australia. He became famous for giving his customers a big smile when he collected their trolley at the Everton Park shopping centre in Brisbane.[77] Even the smallest connection can make a difference.

Aside from a short acknowledgement, your staff should not feel compelled to have an interaction, nor should customers feel compelled to take part in one. If a person doesn't want to interact, that is OK. This can be as simple as a customer who wants to be on their mobile phone while they have items scanned for them at the checkout. The operator shouldn't feel the need to moralise them because they're not interacting with them.

There are hairdressers who offer a service where they don't talk to customers. For many customers, going to a hair appointment is the perfect time to read a book while they're waiting for the hair dye to take. If their preference is to sit quietly, that is OK. An interaction is only valuable if the customer themself values it.

Although it is important to keep in mind that customers may think they don't 'want' an interaction, they may appreciate it when they get one. Often staff members who aren't service minded use this as an excuse, as they don't want to unnecessarily interact with a customer. You'll know either way if a customer appreciates an interaction or not. It's safe to interact and modify it from there.

Like we discussed in Chapter 6, about a job advertisement that asks for problem solving skills, but the position doesn't allow for any problem solving – the same applies here. A job advertisement that asks for exceptional communication skills yet tolerates an absence of communication.

I've said repeatedly that service is not about communication, but communication is essential for an interaction, and an interaction is essential if service is to be done well. Here I'll explore some of the components of an interaction.

Take a moment to think of a fictional character you associate with the word 'curious'. My character is Scooby Doo. Anytime I think of the word curious, he pops into my mind. I remember the cartoons where he and Shaggy are at the tail end of the group, and Scooby sees a tunnel or door and decides to wander in and have a look getting into a spooky situation.

Your character could be Peter Rabbit, Lisa Simpson, Sherlock Holmes, Dora the Explorer or Nemo. Whomever you pick, it might be useful to put an image of them somewhere close by to remind you to be curious. Curiosity fuels interactions.

Let's look at the various components of interactions. First, you need to have the ability to ask questions and not just for the sake of it, but because you are genuinely interested in the response. Good questions can help provoke thought as well as encourage two-way communication. If the service in your organisation is limited to an exchange of one or two words, having more open-ended questions might see a shift in the inter-action. The baseline for an interaction seems to be 'Hi, how are you?' I wonder if this is a real question or someone being polite?

Once you ask a question, you have no choice but to lis-ten. If I asked you whether you believe you're a good listener, what would you say? What about your staff? There are many different levels of listening, and we're often not as good a listener as we might think. Hearing the words are one thing but the emotion behind them is another. Listening is not just about our ears, it's about our whole body – being aware of demonstrating to someone with your body language that you're listening to them.

There is a book called *How to Talk So People Will Listen*, by Steve Brown[78] and a book called *How to Listen So People Will Talk*, by Becky Harling.[79] Talk so people will listen, listen so people will talk. There is a feeling that silence is bad, and that the conversation needs to be kept going, but by slowing down, pausing and using moments of silence in an interac-tion, you can give huge amounts of encouragement to the other person to talk.

Interactions are not always positive and can be challeng-ing. When things aren't going as well as they should for someone, a good interaction involves an apology. As a child we're generally taught to apologise when we've done some-thing wrong, and there are different ways a person can say sorry. With the clients I've worked with, it's been evident that for some, a culture of 'never say sorry to a customer' exists. An apology may not only be about fault; it could also be to apologise for the way someone is feeling.

Some organisations struggle with an apology. If yours does, this short example may help. In 2017, a rail company in Japan apologised after one of its trains departed twenty seconds early. The management on the line between Tokyo and Tsukuba said, 'We sincerely apologise for the inconvenience caused.'[80] While some see this as extreme and highlighting a problem that customers weren't even aware of, it speaks volumes not only about the importance of punctuality, but about the Japanese culture.

Empathy is another component. The ability to communicate that you understand and share the feelings of another person.

Good interactions that go back and forth are great, but often need resolutions. An interaction should help your team problem solve to ascertain what someone wants and think on their feet to find options for customers. An interaction needs an outcome, and if it's hard to get to an outcome, perhaps some further questioning and listening are necessary.

Asking questions, listening, empathising, apologising and problem solving are big ideas, and, for now, it is important that you know what they are and that they form part of an interaction. When they are used effectively in an interaction, the level of service rises significantly. The opposite is also true.

Poor questioning can irritate customers and ignoring a customer can infuriate them. Apologising the wrong way can appear condescending or pitiful. Not having empathy causes a disconnect. Finally, not resolving situations leads to further frustration.

I'm sure you can think of times when you've been a customer and experienced some of these feelings. The world of communication is a complex one and there are subtle things we need to be aware of, not only in our body language, but in our tone and the words used.

There are many things that can affect our communication. Some are barriers in our communication, with others being detractors that effect communication. During the Covid-19 pandemic, public places such as shops and bars installed plastic screens to protect staff and customers. These became barriers to communication as the people behind them (often wearing masks) didn't adjust their volume, which made communicating more difficult.

The pandemic also saw the introduction of proof of vaccine requirements before entering venues, which required staff to add an extra layer of security to police the regulations. Hospitality venues in particular would have positions called 'Covid Marshals' to ensure people were observing the public health protocols. This shift saw a huge movement away from the way people were normally welcomed or greeted into a venue, to a colder and more interrupted reception.

If staff members are not selected appropriately or properly trained, many of these interactions can cause situations to escalate and become adversarial. Even the term 'marshal' brings to mind the image of US law enforcement or a military rank in what would normally be a friendly person greeting people as they enter.

For now, going back to your fictional character, think about how curious you and your team are. Print out a picture of your chosen character and keep it on your desk to remind yourself to be curious when interacting with customers. A curious person is interested to learn so will ask questions and listen to the response. A curious person wants to know if there's a problem and be happy to sympathise and learn more to be able to empathise. A curious person loves to solve problems too and won't give up until they're resolved. Pay attention to your interactions and the interactions your staff members have with their customers.

Leaving positive memories with customers

A positive memory forms when something happens at a deeper emotional level. Positive memories go hand in hand with exceptional service, but many struggle with making them happen for several reasons.

First, when service operates at a higher level of performance in a functional, logical way, the interaction is usually rational. If everything takes place as it's logically expected to, it's unlikely a positive memory will be created because nothing extraordinary happened. That's why a paraprosdokian in comedy is so amusing (when the end of a sentence or joke is unexpected or surprising and requires the listener to reinterpret the first part).

Second, people think that making memories is something that happens continuously. A positive memory only develops when the opportunity presents itself. That's why cliché phrases like 'wowing customers all the time' will never work because it's not a realistic target to achieve. This becomes an issue when staff members don't notice the moment, or even worse – they notice the moment but don't feel empowered to do anything about it.

Having said that, Adam Grant offers a view worth considering, claiming: 'Acts of kindness shouldn't be described as random. They aren't arbitrary or unintentional. They stem from deeply held values or strongly felt emotions.'[81] This is true, so while the opportunity presents itself and the action creates an unexpected positive memory, it is done so by being deliberate.

There is a misconception that positive memories can only develop at places like Disneyland, but that's not true. A positive memory can be created if you work in a law firm, it's just a different type of memory.

A good example to reflect on is what it was like going to the supermarket with your parents when you were a child. When you ask most people the question, the first thing they think of is how boring it was and how they hated it and longed for the day when their parents would be able to leave them at home instead of forcing them to come to the shops. If you look beyond 'going shopping', many memories start to emerge. People recall how they used to play hide and seek. How they'd play hopscotch on the different coloured tiles on the floor. How they used to ride on the trolley. How they used to sneak items into the trolley when the parents weren't looking. How they used to be allowed to put items on the conveyer belt and pay the person at the checkout. Connecting to our childhood memories can put a smile on our face and demonstrate that despite thinking of shopping as boring, there are some golden moments that we cherish too.

In December 2013, Canadian airline WestJet put a virtual Santa Claus in the terminals of Toronto and Hamilton airports and asked passengers on flights bound for Calgary what they would like for Christmas. Unbeknown to the passengers, as they told Santa their wish list, the staff at WestJet were listening and, while the flights were in the air, scrambled to the shops to buy the gifts. Instead of their luggage arriving on the baggage carousel, the customers found wrapped, labelled presents, giving them exactly what they wished for from Santa. The event was filmed and became a viral hit.[82] The sheer surprise and many tears on the passengers' faces demonstrated that the gesture not only had an emotional impact but was something they would never have expected from an airline.

In this example, the memory was powerful not just because of the surprise, but because the airline 'remembered' what they wished for from Santa. There's a clue right there. We previously discussed that memories happen when the opportunity arises, and, sometimes, we can foresee an opportunity to create a positive memory by remembering something ourselves.

Once I was working with a client in the car sales industry, and we discovered that many customers looking to buy an SUV were doing so because they were expecting a child and needed a bigger car for a growing family. We implemented a process (but the customer didn't know it was a process), that if a salesperson knew the couple was expecting a child, they would make a note of it. Then on the day the car was delivered, not only would the salesperson hand the customers their keys, but also give them a set of teething keys for their baby. The customers were surprised and amazed that the salesperson remembered this about them and had waited until the right opportunity (in some cases months later) to create a memorable moment.

People joke about having a poor memory, but as discussed in Chapter 5, remembering details about customers and their situations is far easier when someone is 'being' of service instead of 'doing' customer service. The more present we are, the more we can connect to customers, which allows us to recall information when the opportunity arises.

The point here is that creating a memorable moment is in the delivery. When I purchase a new bottle of aftershave, the server throws a couple of free test samples into the bag.

These accumulate at home and become junk. If the staff member took a moment and framed the sample as a 'gift', it would be more memorable and less likely to be treated as junk.

Let's take the car sales example further. Car salespeople have a negative stereotype attached to them, that they're only nice to get your business and don't care once the car is sold. With this client, we took that stereotype further and set up another process (that the customer was unaware of), where each salesperson would check the daily log of service customers. Whenever a customer came in for their first service, the salesperson would recognise the name and look out for them when they arrived. They would walk up to the customer and say they recognised them and wanted to check in and say hi. This small gesture became memorable, as it changed the negative stereotype and view that customers had of salespeople.

There are many more examples like these, and while the cost involved is usually recouped through the exposure the company receives, there are many things that can work in your organisation for low to no cost. A small handwritten note is a great example.

The good news is that creating a memory is something that can be taught. There are two key strategies that can be used to assist your staff to be memorable. The first is through the customer's emotional journey, and the second is through recovery opportunities. I'll take you through the emotional journey first.

You might be familiar with customer journey mapping, which is used when looking at the overall customer experience by mapping touchpoints, customer channels and the sequence in which a customer interacts with your organisation. The customer's emotional journey doesn't follow touchpoints or channels, but looks at a customer's emotions typically before, during and after their interaction with your organisation. By assessing how customers are feeling at various stages, your staff can look for opportunities that relate to or change a particular emotion the customer is experiencing. This is a useful tool because it challenges the proposition that every customer must be happy when interacting with your staff. This process forces your staff to think about things more from the customer's perspective rather than their own.

American chef Patrick O'Connell owns The Inn at Little Washington in Virginia, and created what he called the Five Stages of Dining.[83] He did this to help his team understand that the experience given to guests is far more significant than just the time they are in the restaurant. The five stages are: anticipation – the moment the customer contemplates a reservation; trepidation – wondering if it will match their expectations; inspection – taking every detail in; fulfilment – getting full, did it meet their expectations; evaluation – was it worth it.

Using these as a basis, I have reworked the five words to make them apply across multiple industries. As I introduce them, I will use as an example a typical customer of an airline, but you can also consider them in relation to your organisation.

1. **Planning**. A family have decided to book a flight three months out for a long-awaited holiday. They're excited about getting to book it and, once they complete their booking, they can't wait for the day to arrive – they wish it was tomorrow.

2. **Preparing**. It's a day or two before their holiday. There is so much to do and they haven't started packing. They get stressed at the last minute and are also worrying about changing a seat at the airport that they're not happy with.

3. **Processing**. The day has finally come, but it's been such a mad rush. They're anxious about getting to the

airport on time and worried they may have forgotten something. The drive to the airport was slow and when they get to the airport, they're concerned about knowing where to queue. They only relax when they get on the plane.

4. **Proclaiming**. With the flight in the air, they finally get excited again. It's been a long time since they were on a plane, and they can't fault the service. Everyone is nice and they're having a great experience.

5. **Perceiving**. As they leave their flight and wait at the baggage carousel, they notice many people are getting their bags quickly and start to worry theirs haven't made it. What if the airline lost their bag? The flight was amazing, but their experience is not over until they get their bag.

This is just an example and there are a few key things to take from it. Firstly, it's not just the one emotion – it's more of a rollercoaster. Secondly, the plane itself only forms one part of the experience – everything else including the traffic on the way to the airport contributes to their emotion. Finally, the person checking them in for their flight cannot assume that they are excited to go on a holiday – while they're excited to go on the holiday, they may not be excited at that moment.

The interaction the check-in agent has with the family is one that could be the best opportunity to create a memory. By being vigilant and noticing the family are nervous, stressed or worried – the staff member could do something to change their emotions. It could be something as basic as 'when you arrive at XX airport, there is a shop right near customs which sells power adaptors for all countries, and it's usually open until every flight clears customs'. This could leave a great memory because it changes the customer's emotion from worry to relief.

A family holiday was used as a storyline for a 2013 ad campaign for accommodation site Booking.com, which depicted a family arriving at a hotel after a horrible ordeal on the flight.[84] It shows that the customer journey does not end at 'perceiving' their travel experience but starts all over again at their accommodation. It's important to consider where your organisation fits in the entire customer journey.

Being memorable is not just about doing big things that customers don't value, but rather doing something small that the customer does value. Thinking of it this way will make the process feel more achievable in the minds of your staff.

The second strategy to create a positive memory is to recover conscientiously when required. A good measure of exceptional service is not only noticing when things are right, but when things go wrong too. Customer recovery is a way to do just that. This is different from conflict management; there may not even be any conflict at this point. Simply, something goes wrong, and your staff should do what's necessary to make it right.

The first type of recovery is called proactive recovery, and this can only happen if the staff member sees an issue before the customer alerts them to it. This is a good thing to train your staff for, and while it's not always possible to see a problem before it's brought to your attention, it's good to be on the lookout.

When an airline knows a bag has missed a flight, the staff will proactively either locate the bag or prepare the report and arrange any compensation while the customer is in the air. When the flight lands they can immediately page the customer and give them any recovery information or compensation and let them be on their way. While the customer will probably still be annoyed that they don't have their bag yet, they will remember the fact that the airline recovered them proactively.

The other example is reactive recovery, and the only difference is this time the customer alerts the staff. While this is usually the more common type of recovery, the positive memory is usually formed based on the speed of the recovery and not the recovery itself.

Using the lost luggage example, if the airline is unaware a bag didn't make it on to the flight, and the customer comes to the baggage counter to report it, the staff member will have to recover the customer reactively. It's an opportunity for them to impress the customer with how quickly they are able to turn it around. This links to what we discussed in Chapter 6 – that discretion must come from an individual without needing to defer to anyone else. In this instance, deferring to another person takes more time and minimises the positive impact on the recovery.

If your staff are recovering two customers that both have the same problem, or the same situation occurs, it is useful to assess separately the impact that the same problem has on each of the customers. Here's another airline example.

There's a daily flight from Perth, Australia direct to London. Imagine the flight is cancelled and two customers approach the counter to express their frustration. The first customer is a frequent flyer in business class who flies this route regularly. She has an important meeting to close a big sale within two hours of the flight's scheduled arrival time. The second customer is eighteen and is travelling on his own to Europe for the first time. He's been saving for this trip for years, and he is due to embark on a tour that departs within two hours of his scheduled flight landing. To be clear, there is no customer more important than another, but when being of service to customers, your staff should be able to ascertain the impacts of a situation to each individual customer.

Here are a few assumptions we could make. The business class customer may be used to delays. She will be able to sit in the comfort of the business lounge while the airline figures out what's going to happen. It's possible that she can call ahead and reschedule the meeting or hold the meeting virtually. The economy class customer hasn't been through this before so he could be anxious. It looks like he'll be sitting on the uncomfortable airport chairs with a voucher for a sandwich. There's no use calling the tour company as their terms state they do not wait for anyone – he will have to make his own way to meet the tour at the next city. Same situation, different impacts. As we get to know our customers more, we can modify our recovery so it's not the same for every customer.

There's a lot to take in here. While it's all about recognising the opportunities, there is always the likelihood that the opportunity is missed. If your team are continuously prepared and operating at this level, the opportunities will appear easier and more frequently. Their luck comes at the intersecting point between being prepared and when the opportunity presents itself. Remember, as educator Dale Carnegie once said, 'When dealing with people remember you are not dealing with creatures of logic, but creatures of emotion.'[85]

QUESTIONS TO CONSIDER

- Do my staff members think about how customers are feeling when they interact with them?
- Are my staff members constantly on the lookout for the right moment or opportunity to create a positive memory for someone?

Deliver an experience that customers want

Fill in the blank of this sentence, 'Customers want a _ experience.' You could put any adjective in the blank to make the sentence complete, but there are two that seem to be at the top of most customers' wish lists. These are: efficient and consistent.

Imagine a customer comes to your organisation for the first time. They get served. Then they come back a second time. This time they hope you remember them from the first time and want their enquiry or service completed efficiently. The customer comes back a third time and, because they have been before, would like their service experience to be consistent with the previous two times. If a customer can receive both efficient and consistent service, and it's convenient for them personally, then you've got a basic but winning formula for keeping your customers happy.

It's not as simple as being efficient and consistent though, because these two create a dilemma as they cancel each other out. Efficient service can be inconsistent, and consistent service can be inefficient. When people think about being efficient, the first thought is to do something quickly, but to be efficient also means to be effective at the same time. The quicker something is done, the greater the chance an error could be made. Time is important for customers, and that's the reason service needs to be thorough – but efficient at the same time.

Take the drive-thru at fast-food restaurants for example. They are probably the most 'efficient' face-to-face businesses. Where else can you get a full meal within minutes without having to leave your car? You place your order at the box, pay at the first window, then pick your order up at the second window. Your order and payment are taken quickly, and the food is handed to you quickly so you can drive off and be on your way. As you leave the drive-thru, you look in your bag and your order is either wrong, missing or lacking in quality. You need to make a decision. Do you drive back around? Go into the restaurant? Or continue on and forget about it?

Efficiency is not just about speed. Speed is one element, but there are three more elements that contribute to efficiency. Ease is the second, accuracy is the third and reliability is the fourth. Putting them all together, efficient service is how quickly something can be done with minimal inconvenience to the customer, delivering the accurate result which can be repeated in this way over a period of time.

Out of these four elements you can see which two are important for the fast-food industry: speed and ease. They are willing to focus on speed and ease but compromise accuracy and reliability as a price. I think fast-food chains know this, and my bet is they don't want to change it. Fast-food chains don't have efficient service; they have efficient processes. A drive-thru is known for being quick and easy. If the restaurants suddenly started slowing service down, even by twenty seconds per car, the impact on the perception of efficiency would be huge. Suddenly, drive-thru wouldn't be an efficient option for customers.

Other businesses can put speed last. If you take Disneyland as an example, everything is easy to find, the service and experience is meticulously planned and it's perfect every time. There's no hiding the fact there are queues and you'll be waiting a long time when you visit, but speed is the price to pay for a greater focus on everything else, and most customers will be expecting the longer wait times.

Speed at a drive-thru and speed at Disneyland are examples of opposite extremes. When it comes to speed in your organisation you should be checking with your customers to see how quickly they want something – remembering that some customers will want things done more quickly than others.

For your organisation, think about these four elements in relation to how efficiently your staff serve customers. Most organisations need to strike a balance between making something quick enough, easy enough, accurate enough and reliable enough to be efficient. If accuracy or reliability start to drop, look at the other two. If speed and ease start to drop, look at the other two and adjust accordingly. Does your organisation have efficient service, or does it have efficient processes?

Consistency is not just about being the same. Let's look at when consistency can become inefficient for customers. When you check-in to a hotel, you are asked for your ID and credit card. If you stayed at the same hotel every month for a year, you'd be asked for these documents each time. This demonstrates that hotels have consistent check-in processes.

As you are a regular customer you wait in line and to go through the same consistent process every time you visit. You would prefer the hotel stored your credit card details and generated an automatic payment so you could go straight to your room. The service you are experiencing is inefficient. The hotel might object, highlighting that they aren't allowed to keep credit card details on file. Other businesses are able to store your credit card details, though, so this should be something which can be looked into to make service more efficient. For example, you can make a purchase on Amazon in one or two clicks.

If consistent service isn't doing the same thing over and over again, what is it? Consistency is about having a consistent eye for detail, being different as you get to know your customers over time, being there for your customers when things don't go well, and looking after them across different departments and teams within the organisation. Too often, an organisation with consistent processes will miss the little details because the process doesn't capture them. They will treat each customer consistently the same way, which will appear robotic.

Many organisations offer consistent service when things are going well but are nowhere to be seen when a problem arises. Full service versus budget airlines is an example. The budget airlines may not have staff in every airport, only operate their call centre during business hours or only have an online option for contact when things go wrong. Most organisations can't promise that things won't go wrong, but do they promise to look after you when things do go wrong?

Finally, it is common to experience consistently great service in one department but not with another. Remember, you may know your organisational structure well, but your customers don't, and they don't care. It shouldn't be a surprise that customers expect to be looked after regardless of the department they are dealing with. A reminder that service isn't always about the outcome, rather how it is handled. It's not about every customer getting what they want every time, it's about them being able to consistently depend on you.

Now that we know efficiency is not only about being fast, and consistency is not only about being the same, we can look at the elements of each and compare these to how we serve our customers. Some processes may need to be redesigned because they can be both inefficient and inconsistent. Customers will expect efficiency and consistency, but you must determine what standard of efficiency and consistency your staff operate when in service to your customers.

QUESTIONS TO CONSIDER

- Do my staff look to make things efficient for their customer?
- Do my staff deliver exceptional service consistently?
- Can our customers count on my staff if they have a problem?
- Do we have standards in place for efficiency and consistency?

PART THREE
EXEMPLIFY

The best thing about a culture of service excellence is that it is noticeable to others, while the work behind it is almost invisible. It's like watching a professional athlete compete in the Olympics. You can see how difficult it is and how well they compete at that level, but you don't see the countless hours of training, hard work, perseverance and effort that go on behind the scenes.

Have you been to a conference where a leader has been invited to speak to showcase their organisation's achievement in a particular area of culture? It doesn't seem to be rocket science, after all you're not hearing anything you haven't heard before, but you ask yourself, 'What's their secret?' Perhaps the word 'secret' is the answer in itself.

Many leaders know the best practices of building a culture of service, but the reality is these best practices are not always commonly practised – or they are practised, but not in alignment with each other. This leads to the constant struggle of putting in effort and seeing no real return.

The final section of this book will delve into what you can do as a leader. This is a step-by-step how-to, bringing best practice into common practice in a way that aligns with everything we have covered so far. It is the role of a leader to exemplify what it means to be of service, and as author Paulo Coelho said, 'The world is changed by your example, not by your opinion.'[86]

SECRET Service

The next six chapters follow a specific sequence, each exploring one element of best practice in detail. It typically follows a path that is known to many as the employee life cycle. You will learn how to exemplify service in an operational way in each of these touchpoints.

Whoever is designated as the best practice project manager, as the leader of the organisation you must understand this process to stay abreast of developments and set the tone for others to follow. The HR department may own these areas, but it's often up to the leaders to run it. Leaders must unite with their HR departments to ensure the best possible outcome for their organisation's service culture.

QUESTIONS TO CONSIDER BEFORE EXPLORING
THIS SECTION:

- **Selection**: Do we select new employees in line with the desired service culture?

- **Education**: Do we implement an induction and ongoing service education initiatives?

- **Conversation**: Do we deliver structured and regular conversations to keep service at the forefront of our employees' minds?

- **Recognition**: Do we recognise service behaviours to encourage ongoing repetition and adoption by more employees?

- **Evaluation**: Do we evaluate our customer service through feedback and continuous improvement processes?
- **Tradition**: Do we make customer service a workplace tradition by treating all colleagues as internal customers?

The SECRET Service model overlays the CABS model, which we explored in Part Two.

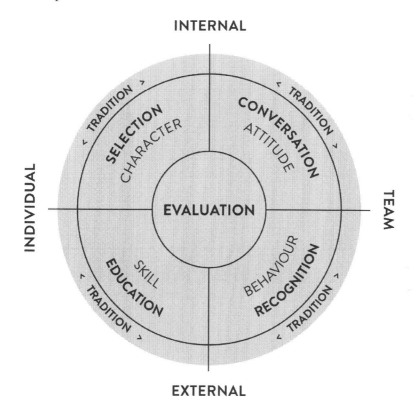

SECRET Service Model

10
Selection

Attract and select in line with the service culture

By now you can see that the choices of words in this book are deliberate. On first glance at this chapter, it's about recruitment, right? Technically it is, but the word 'recruitment' makes me think of enlisting someone into the armed forces, so I've used the word 'selection'.

When you go into a supermarket, you 'select' the items that will go into your trolley. Especially in the fruit and veg department, you browse the display and select the best quality items, leaving the others behind. Sometimes all is not as it seems. Your chosen apple, which looks perfect on the outside, is rotting on the inside, which can only be spotted once cut. You had no way of knowing this, but in most circumstances if you choose wisely, you'll end up with better quality produce.

This analogy applies when bringing in new employees to your organisation. It's the first stage in the employee life cycle and if we can spend more time attracting applicants or candidates that are in line with the desired culture, and selecting those who align, there is a greater chance of hiring a better candidate.

The culture of the organisation is too precious to allow the wrong people to join and potentially destroy the hard work either themselves or by sending the wrong message to the right people already in the organisation. Like the produce example, a selection process can never be 100% effective, but the steps in the life cycle or touchpoints that follow are designed to be a safeguard for the times when the selection hasn't been perfect.

Finding new staff members presents a struggle for leaders. The urgency placed on finding a staff member due to coverage issues can make the process rushed and ineffective. While the process is intended to be about culture, it can quickly become focused on technical skill and the whole recruitment process become a means to an end. When the process doesn't work, a blame game between departments can follow. Managers commonly abdicate their responsibility to HR, and the cycle continues that way.

Do any of these challenges resonate with your organisation? Think about what you currently have in place for attracting and selecting new staff.

There is an abundance of data out there on the cost of poor recruitment practices. Gallup has identified that losing an employee costs the organisation one-and-a-half to two times their annual salary,[87] so it's important to get it right upfront.

If there's one statistic that should be a focus, and that is easily measured, it is the hiring ratio. You get this by calculating the number of total applicants compared to how many positions were offered. The higher the number of applicants per position, the greater the hiring ratio. A greater hiring ratio is an indicator of how selective an organisation can be with who is offered a position.

For example, I was working for an organisation that would employ about 250 people annually, out of over 1,500 applicants. The hiring ratio here was one in six, meaning for every one person selected, six people were not offered a position. There is no specific set ratio. Within that same organisation, the hiring ratio used to be one in two. Fewer applicants meant being selective was more difficult. The difference in culture from a one in two hiring ratio to a one in six hiring ratio was significantly better – and the ratio could continue to climb.

When you refer to the SECRET Service model, you will see that selection sits on top of character. Now that we understand character as the 'giving', 'discretion' and 'effort' required for exceptional service, our selection processes should be about selecting for these three character attributes.

Communicate about the culture in advance

The role of reviewing candidates' job applications is difficult – especially if it's down to just one or two people doing the initial review, which is a glance across the paperwork to see who stands out. It's possible that good applicants are missed during this short process.

If HR teams were to 'gossip' about their job of reviewing candidates, the most common complaint is how candidates don't personalise or follow what is asked of them. I've seen candidates who apply for so many jobs that they don't even take the time to specifically address their cover letter. Or perhaps they send a cover letter used for a previous company without modifying the job title. I once reviewed an application for someone on the customer service desk of a company, whose job application read 'application for chiro-practic assistant'. While this is a red flag to look out for, the same works the other way. If we don't personalise our job advertising, how can we expect those applying to personalise their applications?

This is not designed to be a chapter on copywriting employment ads, but it's important to be aware of some of the pitfalls that can make your advertisement blend in with others. Jargon is one of the biggest pitfalls. Hays Recruitment Director Jason Walker identified the following words to avoid: dedicated, motivated, team player, synergy, leverage, ownership, proactive and reach out.

Australian comedy series *Utopia* is a parody focusing on the lives of employees in a fictional government depart-ment. One scene follows a performance appraisal where the employee mentions the phrase 'task-oriented'. When asked what the phrase means, he responds by saying that he is 'ori-ented to the task'. It would be useful to examine whether your job advertisements contain jargon.

The core goal in marketing to prospective candidates is to specifically communicate as much about the culture of the organisation in advance. When you do this, you are proclaim-ing to any potential candidate what your culture specifically stands for. The more explicit you can make it, the more likely you are to attract applicants who are the right fit for the culture.

There's a local donut shop near me that has an amaz-ing service vibe. When they were recruiting for a new team member, they simply put the following note on their social media page:

'Someone super warm and gregarious to run our till
when the shop is busy. This is the key position when
things are pumping and it's super fun and fast-paced.

Previous hospitality, baking or coffee experience is a plus but not a prerequisite. Looking mainly for that can-do spirit and plenty of warmth.'

The paragraph is to the point but uses relaxed, conversational language that highlights what the culture is like. If you'd been to the store before and read the job advertisement as a candidate, you'd know quickly whether you're the right person to apply for this job. This donut store epitomises exceptional service, and they are clear about the type of person they want to apply.

QUESTIONS TO CONSIDER

- Do we use language in our job advertisements that accurately describes what our service culture is like?
- Do we make our job advertisements stand out so as not to attract more of the same applicants, but more unique applicants?

Showcase the desired culture

I once went into my local supermarket looking for a specific item. It wasn't in stock, and a staff member went to check to see if a load had come in. While I was waiting, my attention was drawn to the front of the store near the checkouts. There was a row of about eight to ten people dressed in black pants and white shirts carrying compendium folders. They looked young (around high school age), and they were standing completely still and silent, hugging their compendiums to their chests. It was clear they were there for either a job interview or their first day induction.

I noticed a staff member who looked like a manager come out of the side office a few times – carrying a clipboard. She powerwalked back and forth in front of these people and clearly was running late and under pressure. Each time she walked past the candidates they looked up at her, but she continued to walk without making eye contact or giving any acknowledgement. Finally, she came back out and said, 'OK, ready, come with me', and the group of people followed her in single file.

Does this sound familiar to what you've experienced in your career? I have been to job interviews where I've sat patiently in reception and watched the disorganisation go on behind the scenes. I have seen the person interviewing asking the receptionist to print something for an interview right in front of me. I've even walked into reception and announced I was there for an interview, which was met by a 'deer in the headlights' moment where the receptionist was obviously unaware that recruitment activity was taking place.

All this day-to-day business in front of prospective candidates shows what the culture is like inside the organisation. Especially when recruiting for service-based roles that are explicit in terms of what is being looked for; these are often completely absent when considered from a candidate's perspective – who is technically a customer at that moment.

Getting a new job and employing someone new is an exciting time. As such, a positive vibe should be created to showcase this to anyone who is not yet employed in the organisation. Pay more attention to make the selection process feel special, without using fakery to lure a candidate in. For example, when I visited the Walt Disney World Casting Centre in Orlando Florida, I noticed the seats in the waiting room all face the centre of the room rather than being set up in rows facing one direction. This way, candidates waiting to be interviewed can look at and talk to each other instead of sitting in silence staring at the front of the room.

One way to ensure this happens is to look at who is involved in your selection process. It is always worth asking someone who is already doing the role (or a similar role) to join the panel. Do you have an employee you wish you could clone ten times over? Ask them to sit in on the interview as their insight will be extremely valuable. You can introduce this person to the prospective candidate to highlight an example of the level of service required and confirm in their minds that the job advertisement was accurate. There is a clear shift here from the interview process being not just about interviewing the candidate, but the candidate interviewing your organisation too.

While this is all about the interview, it extends to day one of employment. I remember when I started a new leadership role, nothing was ready for me when I arrived. No computer access, keys, email or desk. It all fell into place within the first fortnight but did not provide a great welcome on my first day.

Talentica is a software company based in India and is known for a viral video showcasing what they did when their 200th and 201st employee arrived for work on their first day. The entire office welcomed them with a rendition of the hit song at the time, 'Gangnam Style'.[88] This is an example of a way to make new people to the organisation feel welcome – does your organisation do anything similar?

QUESTIONS TO CONSIDER

- Do we give prospective or hired candidates a great impression when they first visit our site?
- Who is involved in our interviews? Do we include any service role models and, if not, can we start to?

A new take on interviews

The interview is often the first and only real chance to have a conversation one-on-one with a prospective applicant. When selecting for a service culture, the questions need to be well thought out so the person conducting the interview can quickly get an idea of whether this person would be a good fit. The interviewee will also get a good understanding of the importance of service within the organisation based on these questions.

It's common for candidates to be nervous when being interviewed, which means they may not showcase their skills or character effectively. The process can be stilted, and if stock questions are asked, the interviewers will get stock answers and the decision made to employ or not is made on limited evidence.

There should be a shift from the interview being conducted like an interrogation to being more of a conversation. Candidates could either receive questions in advance or, more informally, be told what the interview will be exploring. This will help them to respond in a more natural way.

A CEO I know said he would ask candidates a question that they would almost certainly know the answer to. For example, 'What is your favourite colour and why?' If I were asked that question, I would respond, 'Green because when I was in primary school, I was part of the green sports faction, so it became my favourite colour.'

In answering, I shared something personal, and no doubt my face would light up as I reflected on those amazing sports carnival moments in primary school. It's such a great example of how a simple question can bring out a natural reaction – something essential for understanding how someone could 'be' when serving others.

Use the character traits highlighted in Chapter 6 to help you decide on the most effective questions to ask. Take a look at the following questions associated with giving, discretion and effort, and think about how you would answer them if you were interviewing yourself for your current job.

- Tell me of a time when you did something for a customer when you knew you wouldn't get anything back in return.

- Give me an example of when you used your discretion to make a decision that favourably impacted the customer when faced with a difficult situation.

- Can you provide an example of a time when you have put in extra effort even though your workload and other conflicting priorities have made it challenging?

You could turn every point from the character chapter into a question, but the key point here isn't to make it overkill. The three questions above can help distinguish one candidate with these character traits from another.

Everyone needs time to answer the questions, which highlights why it is important to ask the candidate to think about how they would respond to these questions before the interview so you can then have a two-way discussion.

QUESTIONS TO CONSIDER

- Examine what interview questions you currently use – are they effective in getting an insight into whether someone can be of service to others?
- Run the 'reinterviewing' exercise across your organisation – what gold can you identify in your employees' responses? Can you use these as examples during the selection process?

Observations that indicate a cultural fit

In selection, we've moved through how to attract the right person, how to 'be' during the selection process and questions that can help us make informed decisions. Now we will look at how to make an informed decision on cultural fit.

It's great to have all these previous points in place, but if you're unclear of what you're looking for, the candidate is probably unsure too. If multiple people are involved in the selection process, they are all likely to be judging the candidate using different standards, ones that are personal and important to them. This could lead to an inconsistent selection process.

When you're interviewing, it can be useful to imagine the candidate working in your organisation and serving your customers. Does it look and feel good? What is your intuition saying?

Delta Airlines includes the following question in their customer survey, based on an interaction between a customer and staff member in the call centre: 'How likely would you be to hire the last Delta representative you talked to, if you ran a customer service company? 1, no, to 5, yes, definitely.'[89] While Delta's question is more around service feedback, if you knew it was going to be asked down the line, then it's certainly something you would consider when deciding to hire a person or not.

When I think about the most powerful service moments in shopping centres or tourism attractions, how the staff assists in situations with lost children is top of the list. I take Delta's question above to a different level and would ask, 'Would this person make a lost child comfortable when searching for their parents?' and 'Would this person make a frantic parent comfortable when searching for their child?' These are useful questions to reflect on as it keeps the focus in selection based on how someone would 'be' in that moment compared to what they would 'do' in that moment.

You can't make using these questions the way to make decisions – they are examples to help orientate your thinking when conducting interviews. There are, however, four key areas that can be used and communicated in advance to tell candidates what you are looking for. These four areas are observable in the interview process as well as if you were watching one person serve another. A useful way to remember this is with the formula $P^2 + C^2$. This stands for presentation, participation, communication and confidence. They are a guide to support your decision on whether a candidate meets or does not meet your selection criteria. It shifts your team's focus on to something more evidence-based rather than relying on gut instincts.

1. **Presentation** – how does the person present themselves? It's not about dressing formally or too casually, but rather, do they present themselves well overall? Are they putting their best foot forward for you as the interviewer, which they should also do for their customers? Did they turn up prepared and organised?

2. **Participation** – have they actively participated in the selection process? This is particularly useful for group interviews but also applicable in one-on-one interviews. In a group format, do they listen to the instructions given for the activity and do they persist in and contribute to discussions with other candidates? Does the person use the interview process as a way to gain an insight into your organisation, or do they sit back and let you do the heavy lifting? Do they make it easy handing you the documentation required, or do you constantly need to ask for things?

3. **Communication** – can they communicate well? We've talked before about service not only being about communication, but communication being an important part of service. If you give the person a good chance to showcase their best self, you will be able to determine their communication ability.

4. **Confidence** – this is not about the candidate being a confident or extraverted person. Rather, do they give you confidence that they can do their job with customers? Do they seem genuinely interested in service and other people, or does it appear they are going through the motions to get the job?

Ensure that these four standards are in place in your organisation and are especially demonstrated by those involved in the selection process. You can't expect it from candidates if the people interviewing them don't display them either.

QUESTIONS TO CONSIDER

- Are we clear on exactly what our organisation is looking for during the selection process?
- On reflection, how have recent candidates we have employed measured against presentation, participation, communication and confidence in their interviews?
- Have there been any red flags missed during the interviews that you can see in hindsight?

11
Education

Implement a service education program

In some organisations, training a new staff member can be viewed as something on a checklist with no real value placed on it. There's little focus on the difference thorough training can make; instead it centres on technical rather than emotional elements. This is often the only training a new staff member will get.

When little focus is placed on training new staff members, any candidates that 'slipped through' the selection process go unnoticed as the training is not thorough enough to be a secondary safeguard to the poor selection decisions. Does any of this sound like the culture of training in your organisation?

Training has been seen to relate to skill. However, what comes before training? While I think training skills are important, the concept of education is certainly missing, especially from a culture and service perspective. If training is about the skills and 'doing', then the education should be around the theory and 'being' that sits behind this.

When you look at the SECRET Service model, you will see that 'education' sits on top of skill. We're not moving in a clockwise direction, but moving from up to down, then left to right. Even though education is regularly group based, you're connecting learning points with each person as an individual.

Although training covers the main practicalities, it can sometimes leave smaller details unaddressed.

In the 1990s, the American fast-food pizza company Little Caesars launched a marketing campaign promoting their home delivery service. The commercial was set at a fictional training facility in the middle of the Gobi Desert where new pizza delivery drivers were being trained.[90] I ask people to tell me the steps they need to know to deliver a pizza – such a simple task that stumps people with the 'steps' involved. The humorous ad shows the drivers being trained on how to close their car door, how to avoid a dog chasing them, how to avoid garden sprinklers from soaking the pizza, how to climb the stairs to the front porch, how to knock on the door and how to ring the doorbell. While it's another example of clever advertising, it does show the detailed steps involved in completing a task – something that is missed by many training programs. It highlights that when training doesn't capture the issue the staff member is dealing with, they need to fall back on their education to figure out what must be done.

A 2019 study by Talent LMS found that in food and beverage businesses, an alarming 70% of employees in customer-facing roles did not receive any customer service training.[91] This statistic could highlight the degree that being able to serve a customer is 'implied' rather than known and understood by both the organisation and the employee.

An induction as an education initiative should be the first touchpoint when someone joins an organisation, and it's the second touchpoint after selection in the employee life cycle. It is the perfect situation to reinforce the culture of the organisation set during the selection process and to make sure that if anyone 'slipped through' they can see this explicitly and self-select out of the process themselves, or be identified and monitored by the person who is facilitating the induction.

Another CEO I know, would refer to the induction process as 'inductrination' – a play on the word indoctrination used by the leaders of the organisation to give the induction added importance. The induction is about inculcating a person and culture together.

Inductions can be mistaken as being the same as orientations, which are designed to 'orient' new staff to the organisation. An orientation shows staff where the staff room is, allocates them a locker, shows them where to park and where to view their rosters. These are important questions that a new staff member cares about, but we will shortly talk about when to schedule this conversation.

The Walt Disney Company calls the inductions for new cast members at Disneyland 'Traditions'. The Traditions program is attended by everyone at every level who joins the organisation. Here they learn about the foundations of the Disney culture as well as the language, symbols, values, standards and behaviours, and how the excitement about working for Disneyland is generated. It takes a full day to complete the program and must be done on the cast member's first day of work – no exceptions.[92]

I see staff members on induction programs that are held a month after they joined the company. This happens because there is not enough emphasis placed on the importance of the induction. If it is viewed as essential, no employee should be working in the organisation without it.

Other global world-class service brands are no exception. At Zappos, all new staff members regardless of level must complete the same training that is given to call centre repre-sentatives. This is a four-week program with two weeks on the phone taking calls from customers. At the end of the first week, the entire class are offered $2,000 to quit to make sure that they are there for more than just a pay check. On average, less than 1% take up the offer.[93] If your organisation chose to implement something like this, it would be in addition to what we discussed in Chapter 7 where senior leaders spend one day every few months working on the frontline.

At The Ritz-Carlton Hotel, all team members must com-plete a twenty-one-day certification training program before they are able to work with guests. The Ritz-Carlton also requires their staff to complete 250 hours of training and pro-fessional development each year.[94]

The point is not to emulate a three-week program because The Ritz-Carlton does but to highlight how these global brands that are renowned for their service do not leave anything to chance and ensure that education initia-tives are built in and not negotiable. You may have heard the saying 'quality over quantity' before, and when it comes to service education, sure there have been sessions that have run too long and things can be simplified. The one thing this book illustrates, though, is how deep service can be. When something has depth, it requires time. A quick hour of a service induction will not prepare your team for what they need to succeed in service.

The induction should be the first of many service initia-tives. You can be inducted to an organisation when you start, but it can be reinforced many times during a person's employ-ment. A memorable induction without any formal follow-up training shows that the induction was not as important as it was made out to be. We'll talk more about the frequency of education initiatives later in this chapter.

Maximising a return on investment

Service education is a cost to the business, although it shouldn't be seen this way. Some of the biggest obstacles that get in the way are not being able to justify a return on investment of service education; a view that the education program itself is the solution and not part of the solution; and that the education program is not supported both before and after it has taken place.

A service education program is never done to get 'business as usual' as a result. The program is about change and bringing about change in the workplace. One of the biggest underlying obstacles is that people in your organisation may be open to education but may not be open to change. These two things go hand in hand. You can't have one without the other.

When I introduced this section of the book, I talked about best practice versus common practice. It's easy to put together a service culture induction and follow-up program because it's important. Many people do not understand that the formal education component is merely an 'event' among a whole tonne of hard work. It's the before and after parts of the actual education program that require the most attention. At the minimum here are a few things that need to be conveyed not only by yourself as the leader, but those who are directly influential to new staff.

Before any formal service education program, leaders must be able to sell the benefits of it to the person and the organisation. This stops people wondering why they are doing it and adopting the attitude that they know everything before giving it a go.

Leaders must also be encouraging to those attending. It is common to hear of leaders who see programs like this as an interruption to their team and can sometimes actively try to stop participants from attending. I've seen the excuse 'end of month reporting' used at every stage of a month. In other words, there's not a good time for a person to be released on to a program.

Finally, notice is important. For recurring education initiatives, leaders actively need to allow their staff to attend by alleviating that day's duties. If a staff member attends an education program but is thinking about the work and deadlines they will return to the next day, their minds will be distracted, and the program is a redundant exercise. You need to make room for the program – note that making a staff member start at 5am to clear some work before attending a program at 9am is not effective.

After the program ends there are important things to consider. The leadership team must make those who have attended an inspirational education session feel comfortable to put the things they've learned to good use when they return to their work.

The first element is to hold their team to account once they get back to work. The hardest part of change is not learning what to change but sticking to it once the learning is done. Making sure that things don't go back to 'the way things were' is the biggest pitfall and can destroy the efforts of education initiatives.

The final element is to ensure that there are risk-free opportunities for your staff member to test out. Training is usually undertaken when work is quiet, followed by a busy period as soon as it's completed. We'll talk specifically on scheduling soon, but it is the role of a leader to make sure they don't just hold their teams to account, but also to modify the work environment for new learnings to be tested and reinforced. The term 'baptism of fire' is joked about, but, if it can be avoided, there will be a greater return on investment.

QUESTION TO CONSIDER

- Do your leaders actively support their people attending education initiatives before and after the learning program?

Building content into the program

Imagine you're sitting in your office with a blank sheet of paper ready to populate the ideas for content to be included in your organisation's service and culture education program. It's a big task.

You must not only think of what is most important to communicate, but also how to communicate it in an elegant and engaging way. You need to connect learning to future learning without coming across as patronising or condescending to those who have already 'done it before'.

Understanding the value of service education and getting the buy-in from your leaders is one thing, but being able to come up with content is what will determine whether your program takes off, or if it becomes that thing where you tried once and it never worked. Once you've got the content ideas the work isn't over; the task then becomes to flesh out those ideas and make them relevant for those who will learn from the program. Once you have the ideas, the rest flows much easier.

It's impossible at this level to tell you what to include specifically in your service culture education initiatives, but if in this chapter I can help with the ideation part, most of the work is done. Fortunately, there is a formula that I've covered in this book already. This section should be read in conjunction with Chapter 9 – Skill. Everything in Chapter 9 would traditionally be the basis and structure to follow for your education initiative. You can see the overlap of education and skill in the SECRET Service model.

To recap the four key parts of Chapter 9:

1. **Deliberately** making service a reason for coming to work is all about the 'why'.

2. Developing connections through customer **interactions** is all about the 'who and how'.

3. Leaving positive **memories** with customers is all about the 'when and where'.

4. Delivering **experiences** that customers want is all about the 'what'.

The point here is not how long you spend on a program, it's the flow of information that best resonates with your people. While not identical, the flow of these four areas is similar to Bernice McCarthy's '4MAT Learning Model' developed in the 1980s.[95] This not only considers different learning styles, but also ensures the process of learning is complete by flowing across more than one style.

Starting with the 'why' explores the purpose and why service is important. Unpacking this reason specific to your organisation will give your staff meaning and put intent behind everything they do.

The 'who and how' is about who your customer is and how to serve them. What are your signature service standards? How do you expect the interactions with your customers to be? Introduce the specific tools you use to help build relationships and make meaningful connections during service interactions.

The 'when and where' is about looking for the opportunities and moments that will make a difference. Look for a range of situations that your team may be exposed to and finish this sentence: When this happens you could do this. . .

Finally, the 'what' is about what to do to create the best experience for customers. In Chapter 9, we explored serving efficiently and consistently. This last part is impossible without the previous three. You need to know the reason behind something, how to interact with a customer and when to make the best difference possible before you focus on the way you work. Being efficient by not interacting, not creating a positive memory and not thinking about the intent behind your job is rudely rushing a customer. Or being consistent without everything else is being robotic.

For any program – regardless of length – using these four focus areas is the best way to come up with your own content. Participants will not learn quickly if content has been taken from other companies because it won't relate or connect at the level you want it to. Inductions are seen as 'much of a much-ness'. If your organisation is to be renowned for their service and culture, making an induction unique is the first step to standing out on someone's first day at work.

If you spend time exploring the different things in each heading, you will come up with more content than you need. This makes it easy to decide what content is important for day one and what could be used in subsequent ongoing learning programs.

Don't make the mistake of thinking the induction is the place to cram everything in and potentially overload the inductees. It's no wonder that when there is so much training people forget the basics like service. The inductees should finish their induction feeling more comfortable about working with you, not inundated and overwhelmed. The messaging at the induction should be higher level, with the more practical elements to follow in subsequent training. To quote poet Johann Wolfgang von Goethe, who said 'you really only know when you know little. Doubt grows with knowledge.'[96]

It is likely that these further elements and other specific topics will come up throughout the year and will warrant some additional time and attention. This doesn't necessarily need to be formal training sessions; they can be captured in service conversations, which we will discuss in the next chapter.

I have tried to not be specific in terms of how long an induction should run, but you need to be realistic with a starting number. Looking at the four parts from earlier in this section (deliberate, interactions, memorable, experiences), spending at least an hour on each would equal a half day for an induction. This should be the minimum time allocated with the option for more if needed.

QUESTION TO CONSIDER

- In hindsight, what do you wish you knew about your organisation that should have been covered in your induction?

Determine the scheduling and frequency

We've explored the concept that simple is not easy. This theme certainly runs through this chapter. Just when you've finished reading about ideating new content comes another hurdle – scheduling in the education initiatives.

It's a hurdle for every business. I haven't met an organisation that has a calendar which allows for easy release of staff for training. Even the quietest times of the calendar year are filled with other long-term projects and annual leave. In other words, operationally, there's never a good time to schedule in learning. It would be quite contradictory for a customer service learning program to get in the way of delivering service to customers, but it has to happen.

Before we look at the ongoing education initiatives, let's just start with the induction first. When someone starts a new job, there's a lot to get through. There's the orientation part (discussed earlier) as well as the safety and compliance part of onboarding, covering manual handling, fire and emergency exits, and the alcohol and drugs policies. Finally, there is the service and culture element.

Most organisations allocate one block of time to cover all these aspects. This is not a question of whether service is more important than safety – they are both important. Putting them together out of convenience does more harm than good – it dilutes both messages. The biggest thing to consider when delivering a service induction is to run it separately from everything else. Even if you only have one hour allocated to it, run that hour in isolation or cover the culture content on a separate day.

This approach may cost more in labour and logistics, but in the long run the attention it will be given will far outweigh any costs associated. It's important to also clarify how to roll out 'on-the-job' service training when frontline team members join the business. Let's take using a cash register as an example. Many organisations put people on to the cash register and have a more experienced person watch over them for their first week. While the support is great, the new team member has to juggle learning the register with practising their service.

A key idea to implement is that, for the first week, the team member only interacts with the customer (while the support person presses all the buttons on the register), so they get used to the service element before they work on the technical elements. New staff members struggle with this initially because of the sheer pressure of customers standing in front of them. Once they are comfortable with customers, they can practise on the cash register.

Learning maths at school is a great comparison – albeit a simplified one. When we start school, we learn how to count one through to ten. Yet, maths class continues for one hour a day for the remaining twelve years of schooling, continuing to build on your skills and knowledge, but essentially relying on those numbers one through to ten. Service is the same. There are some core principles that can be covered in an induction, but the opportunities to build on the principles are endless.

In the 1980s and 1990s, American researchers developed a 70:20:10 model for learning and development.[97] Despite various criticisms over the years, the model has stuck. It outlines that most learning (70%) comes from on-the-job experiences, 20% from feedback, and 10% from formal courses and reading. This means that the formal nature of learning initiatives does not make up a huge component of the annual calendar, so I'm not suggesting letting it take over. At the minimum, I am suggesting there should be two touchpoints per calendar year where your people formally come together to focus on service education. The duration is entirely up to you, but the scheduling and frequency is most important.

A few years ago, I was planning some service sessions with the owner of a fish market. I was asked the question, 'When is the best time to run the sessions?' I responded, 'Once the week before Christmas, and once in the middle of

June.' The Christmas suggestion was the most shocking. For international readers, Christmas in Australia is in the middle of summer and seafood is in season. On Christmas Eve, news reports show queues of people lining up from as early as 4am to get their seafood on days when the weather is in the high thirties. At certain times in June, you could find yourself as the only one in the fish market. The type of service received at a seafood market on Christmas Eve will definitely be different to the service received in June. Neither should be better or worse, just different. The same goes for retailers with the Boxing Day sales compared to the quiet parts of the year where sales are slow.

A focus on bringing everyone together for formal service education right before customers (and their expectations) ramp up will ensure that your people are prepared for the change in operating climate and will adjust their service accordingly. Bringing everyone together when times are slower allows a greater focus on relationship building, possibly even more sales. There is time to interact with each customer and an opportunity to learn new skills, as the mind isn't inundated as it would be at other, busier times of the year.

Inviting all staff to service education initiatives twice each year is important, but there's one group that needs to be catered for separately. For every new staff member who joins the organisation, following their induction, there should be some form of ongoing coaching and follow-up within the first ninety days of their employment.

According to Harvard Business School career coach Matthew Spielman, 'Research suggests that an employee's first ninety days will in large part determine his or her performance, longevity, and contribution to the company.'[98] This is probably why a probationary period lasts for three months.

It wouldn't require a formal training day, but if there was some sort of progressive on-the-job learning program that new staff completed over the course of their first few months, it would mean that the standalone induction wouldn't be packed with too much information. It could be more impactful at a high level and supported by the on-the-job learning.

Take a moment to think about all of the content and time required to spend on education and training for your staff members. Once they've received the required knowledge just think how valuable they will be in service to customers. The gap between what a staff member knows and what a customer knows would be huge – yet many organisations continue to place more onus on their customers. We discussed the concept of self-service in Chapter 1, so it's a good idea when looking at this part of the book to segment some of the steps or skills that you may expect customers to complete, and then ensure that your staff are trained on these to support them as they provide a human touch to anything automated.

QUESTIONS TO CONSIDER

- Are your people prepared to serve differently at different times of the year as well as in the event of a crisis like a global pandemic?
- When is the busiest time of year for your organisation?
- What things could you consider that would improve the service experience for customers and staff members during busy periods?
- When is the quietest time of year for your organisation?
- What things could you consider that would improve the service experience for customers and staff members during quiet periods?

Picking your facilitator

Let's talk about some of those 'horrible' training moments. You know the ones where the facilitator arrives a few minutes before it starts. They're fumbling with their computer cables, and you can see their anxiety rising. Then they start, and you find them completely uninspiring, but you politely tick the 'outstanding box' on your feedback form to avoid an awkward confrontation.

This section is about shifting the energy in the room from 'not another day of training' to 'this is amazing!' If there are only two times each calendar year, aside from the induction, to focus on service culture education, there's only those two times to get it right. It comes down to the person facilitating that makes the difference. This leads me to ask, who facilities the service culture education in your organisation, and, if there isn't anyone currently, who will you pick?

The world of organisational training and development has a few negative stigmas associated with it. Typically, in larger organisations I have seen trainers selected in the following ways. The first is picking one of the longest serving people in the organisation. They've been around a while, and they know everything – they'd be the best person to impart their knowledge. Or the second is picking a person who is on 'light duties' who is being transitioned out of an operational role to a more administrative role and taking on the portfolio of training. I'm not saying that someone who is long serving or on light duties doesn't have any value to give, but these two choices are not necessarily the best person to facilitate a program in an inspirational way for others to follow.

There can be many talented people in the organisation who would be outstanding facilitators but are overlooked because of the dated perception that they are not suitable to deliver training. Equally the 'fresh kid' who can capture an audience will still have to gain trust from their peers, but the point here should be about the person that is best suited to deliver an engaging session.

Back to the Disney example. Facilitators of the Traditions program are selected through an extensive audition process and teach the course a few times throughout the year. There is a pool of experienced facilitators who can cover for sickness and annual leave, so courses are not delayed or cancelled.

There is a difference from someone internal delivering programs to engaging someone externally. For instance, I am often engaged by organisations to either complement the internal facilitators or replace an internal facilitator if there isn't anyone suitable to deliver with the required impact. It's great when an organisation realises their limitations in training and opts for quality over settling for second best.

Anyone who facilitates a learning program should be able to do three things, just like the three parts of this book:

1. **Excite** participants about service culture and bring enthusiasm to the program.

2. **Encourage** participants – while learning can be fun, it's also serious. Someone who is patient who can help participants on their learning journey will be a great asset.

3. **Exemplify** what it truly means to be of service. Trainers can cop a lot of criticism from participants, especially those 'do as I say, not as I do' types. The person at the front of the room must be a role model or risk jeopardising the entire learning opportunity.

These three traits are more important than the way the content itself is delivered. What happens is organisations fall into the trap of developing stringent learning guides that give a minute-by-minute breakdown of how to run a session, which is criticised by anyone who facilitates the program because they interpret it differently.

While there should be key messages that must be delivered consistently, the focus of picking a facilitator is more about how they bring their own uniqueness to the delivery and getting them to deliver an inspirational program in a way that will not seem robotic and clunky.

QUESTIONS TO CONSIDER

- Are your current learning programs around service and culture inspirational and influential to those who attend?
- Whom do you currently use to facilitate service culture programs? Do they meet the excite-encourage-exemplify criteria?

12
Conversation

Keep service at the forefront of minds

As a leader, delivering structured and regular conversations is the best way to keep service at the forefront of minds. The previous two chapters have explored two isolated events at the beginning of the employee life cycle – selection and education.

While these structured events are important, if you look at where most of the time is spent, there is space that needs to be filled by leaders to ensure that service doesn't drop off the radar. In Chapter 11 I introduced the 70:20:10 framework for learning and development. This chapter is where the 70% covered on the job comes into practice. You may ask, if we hire the right people with character and train them well, why would service drop off the radar without the constant reinforcement? Being of service requires a lot of work, and you may have some people in your organisation who never need reminding. These are your top service performers, but not everyone fits into this category.

People are only human, and while people don't become less skilled at service, it can be easy to be defeated and lose focus. When you look at the SECRET Service model you will see that 'conversation' sits on top of 'attitude'. If you recall Chapter 7 – Attitude, we explored the key challenges and obstacles in a workplace that can be destructive to attitudes. While Chapter 7 gave key strategies to overcome the obstacles thrown at us, regular conversations about service with your entire organisation keeps these attitudes fresh and front of mind.

The workforce can lack open and honest communication. Messages are diluted by noise, and people are strapped for time. When we look at the bulk of in-person communication, it's usually formal like a meeting and treated like a briefing – one way. Think about a time that you've been involved in a work-related conversation and how different this feels from sitting in a meeting.

When most organisations encounter a service-related crisis, they jump at the chance to communicate with their staff, but only once. The lack of follow-up communication then leads to mixed messaging and confusion.

As a leader, having structured and regular conversations about service sends clear and powerful messages to the greater team about its importance to the organisation. This is essential in gaining maximum support and cultural buy-in from the team.

It is interesting that the mining industry values safety so much that they have widespread 'safety minute' meetings before the commencement of work each day, and this is part of the culture. How good would it be if 'service minutes' operated in the same way in your organisation?

When it comes to conversations, the biggest problem a leader faces is keeping these conversations consistent and regular. This is because they are treated too formally. We will explore having formal meetings later in this chapter, but, for now, the conversations discussed here are informal catch-ups. These can also be referred to as 'huddles'. The implementation point here is to start a regular 'huddle' at the beginning of each shift (or a week at least) that can keep service in the forefront of minds, just like safety huddles keep safety a core focus.

In Chapter 5, we explored the definitions and common mistakes of service cultures. We discussed that one pitfall of trying to change attitudes is to convince people. Conversations are different to convincing. A conversation is about encouraging their participation in the discussion to gain the support that's required, not using the first few minutes of each shift to bark orders at your staff.

Messages are continually being transmitted about your attitudes toward service, so it's worth keeping that in mind during your regular informal conversations or huddles. Avoid being the leader that holds regular service conversations but does everything else contrary to the spirit of the conversation.

QUESTIONS TO CONSIDER

- Review the current conversations you hold about service. How frequently do you communicate with your teams?
- Is this communication formal or informal?
- Are your conversations regular or sporadic?
- Can you see a service huddle taking place at the beginning of each shift (or each week depending on your business operation)?

Develop topics for conversations

On 8 October 1992, US President George HW Bush proclaimed to Congress that the first full week of October would be National Customer Service Week.[99] The celebration has grown internationally and is recognised by organisations globally.

Like with any week of reflection, they are useful in drawing special attention to a worthwhile topic or cause, but they are only useful if they are remembered in the remaining fifty-one weeks of the year. As customer service is the way we are 'being' every day when we are at work, having one week annually to think about it is not enough. It must be talked about all year.

Similar to the previous chapter when we discussed ideating content for education, the same challenge exists in developing topics for regular service conversations. The difference with a conversation is they are far more casual and shorter, and the focus must be narrower. This means that developing topics should be easier.

A few years ago, I printed a small handbook for my clients. It was called *52 Customer Service Conversations* and it consisted of just that – fifty-two conversation starters about customer service. When I picked the books up, the server in the print shop told me he liked the book and that, because many of the conversations seemed basic in nature, the book would be a quick reference tool to flick through. It was then that I picked one of the conversations and showed him how profound it was. A conversation topic seems basic in nature, but once you get discussing it, you can see its full potential.

I developed another book that had double the amount of conversation starters. That's two years' worth of weekly conversations generated by taking several key words (many which are used in this book) and opening up a conversation about what they mean. The 'questions to consider' in this book will be enough to have robust conversations with your leadership team (note, they're not designed for conversations with the wider team).

Having conversations about service based on a weekly theme is a great way to keep the topic of service alive on a long-term basis. It's important to remember not to fill the diary completely, as other conversation topics will come up. For example, in many industries, customer service messaging will change around marketing campaigns such as Valentine's Day, Mother's Day, Father's Day and other similar events. It's important to have conversations around serving customers during these times. Having a regular time to talk about service means that when issues arise, you already have a regular and prebooked spot where your team can expect you or other leaders to discuss them.

There are many organisations that have brilliant marketing, but the staff delivering service have no idea what's written on the company's website or offers aren't updated on the point of sale. This is not about picking on the marketing team, but looking at some of the general challenges faced by staff each day and creating a safe environment in which to talk about them.

Consider the following questions to encourage discussions about service with your teams.

- What about service do you find the most difficult?

- Are there things that customers find out before you do? How do you feel when you're faced with this situation?

- Do you know how the business is tracking in terms of customer service?

Lunchrooms can be a breeding ground for gossip. Sometimes the things that staff discuss in the lunchroom (which may be seen as complaining) are the perfect topics to identify for discussion more frequently. The staff on the frontline are dealing directly with customers every day – they'll be your best source of conversation topics.

When topics are aligned to the issues that your staff may be facing, a shift begins to develop. There will be less struggle and less feeling of being excluded, unnoticed, unempowered and uninvolved.

While on the topic of inclusion, the more complex your organisation's rostering is (especially if there are rotating day and night shifts), the longer each topic of conversation must run for. The biggest mistake is having the conversations only in the morning and the night shift missing out, or having the conversation for one week but changing topics when a new team is rostered for the following week. Each topic must be heard and discussed by everyone to achieve inclusion. Keep these conversations brief – a minimum of five minutes, maximum of fifteen – and have them once a week to keep a weekly theme and focus area alive.

Implement a formal customer service meeting

Regular conversations at staff level is one thing, but leaders must also take the time to discuss the service in the organisation formally. While this isn't a book on effective meetings, I hear the same from many leaders: there are too many meetings, and they don't seem to be effective. This is not about adding a meeting to a busy calendar, but it is about examining how much time your leadership team spend away from the things that add value to your customers (or their customers).

In Chapter 7, we discussed how a perceived lack of time and resources is used as an excuse why things can't be done, so I expect that in line with that chapter, some efficiencies in time will have already been made. This section is about meeting with your leadership team to talk about customer service at a more strategic and formal level, compared to the informal huddles with the wider and frontline team that take place more frequently which we explored earlier in this chapter.

The late Sir Peter Blake was a New Zealand yachtsman who led the national team to successive wins in the America's Cup. He was known for his ability to focus his team on one single strategic question: will it make the boat go faster?[100] When it comes to customer service, every organisation should have a similar question: can we serve our customers better?

Most leaders meet regularly for a 'management meeting'. The first step is to change the title of the recurring invitation and call it a 'customer service meeting'. A small change like this can make a huge difference, as it will set the tone for what the meeting should be about.

Given that most organisations experience the same challenges that we discussed in Chapter 7, the theme of each obstacle can be an agenda item:

- **Alignment**: Are there any conflicting messages out there that make our team believe that service is less of a priority?

- **Credibility**: How often have leaders spoken about customer service to their staff members in the past week/month?

- **Time and resources**: What is getting in the way of delivering better service to our customers?

- **Clarity**: How are we tracking in terms of noticeable improvements to our service culture?

- **Change**: Have we noticed any of our customers' needs and expectations changing?

There should be one more item added, and this is to discuss staff feedback. We've already acknowledged that the staff on the frontline who actively engage with customers daily are an amazing source of feedback.

Most leaders will have heard of the staff 'suggestion box' in the lunchroom that never gets checked. Well, it's now time to revive it. The box should ask for suggestions to improve the service experience for customers (or customer experience in general). Each item should be read out at the leadership customer service meeting with the response written and circulated back to the staff on the frontline. This shows them that the suggestions are being read, considered, implemented or not implemented, which will increase the quality of subsequent recommendations put forward. The more connected the staff on the frontline are to their customers, the greater chance a simple idea may well be the source of improvement to the overall customer service of the organisation.

Discuss customer feedback

While on the topic of conversations, there needs to be a closed loop link that ensures the incoming customer feedback can be shared with staff members on the frontline. This section is about making customer feedback a topic of conversation which applies to both positive and negative feedback. It's particularly important to mention positive customer feedback as you don't want to give the impression to your staff that only negative feedback is discussed with them. It's the positive feedback that can lead to some of the greatest improvements in culture.

I've spent most of this chapter presenting the case for regular conversations. Regrettably, feedback in general is not fed back, and only brought up at certain times of the year – usually in performance conversations. When it comes to scheduling the sharing of customer feedback, there is no better time to do it than when it comes in (or as soon as possible after). For this section, we will explore positive feedback first, then in Chapter 14 discuss the steps for dealing with negative feedback.

Sharing verbatim negative feedback publicly, even with the names omitted, creates finger pointing and possible shaming. If there are negative issues to raise in conversation, they are best done in a general way only. When discussing positive feedback written by a customer, this should be read out loud verbatim in front of the entire team. This is not only to publicly congratulate those involved, but to share how the collective efforts of improving a service culture led to an increasing amount of positive written feedback.

When I was a leader in an organisation, I was asked by a fellow manager for some tips on running an engaging morning briefing session. I printed some positive feedback written by a customer and asked the manager to take it with him and spend time that afternoon reading it before sharing the verbatim feedback the following morning.

I see leaders take notes they are given and try to make them conversational by skipping bits and pieces, but when a customer takes time to give positive feedback, they write with emotion. They give the detail of what happened and how it made them feel. To paraphrase or summarise what they've written will completely lose the desired impact compared to reading it verbatim out loud.

I told the manager to read the feedback the following morning like he was performing a script on a stage play, and I gave him four key strategies to ensure he delivered a powerful and memorable briefing. These same four strategies apply to you and your leaders reading out positive feedback in their briefings.

1. **Rehearse the lines**. Close the office door and read it to yourself out loud. Learn and perfect the pronunciation of key words, long words, names and surnames. Read it that many times that you have almost memorised it.

2. **Internalise each word**. Feel the emotion that the words evoke and say them like you are experiencing them yourself.

3. **Read with passion**. This creates the same level of excitement that would exist if the customer themselves was called in to deliver the feedback to the team.

4. **Project so everyone can hear**. We've all been part of a briefing were the volume decreases as the brief goes on. Noise and distractions may exist, so reading feedback must be done so that everyone, especially at the back, hears it.

Make sure the same piece of feedback is read multiple times over a week and during various shifts, so everyone has chance to hear it. It's better that one person hears the same feedback three times than another person missing it full stop. It will also be helpful to make a video to include remote teams, or you could hold online conferencing briefings simulating an in-person setting.

When I suggest regular conversations to organisations, they often tell me that feedback is circulated via email, or print, which is pinned on the lunchroom noticeboard. This is not enough as it leaves it to individual staff members to read it. You will not be able to control how they interpret it, so it may not have the same impact than if it were read to them.

One of the key things to emphasise when discussing positive feedback isn't so much what specifically happened, as this could potentially send the wrong message to replicate that same situation, which may not be appropriate or work. Rather, it is to have a discussion around how positive moments make customers feel and that they are not always 'trained' and instead done spontaneously. You may find that the positive compliments you receive have not been trained to your staff members (otherwise everyone would be doing them), so you want to emphasise the initiative shown by the staff member first and what they specifically did.

QUESTIONS TO CONSIDER

* Do we share positive stories of great service across the organisation?
* Are our leaders well equipped to run briefings and conversations in a powerful way?

Be relentless in your communication

Relentless is a powerful word that I love to use. I was once facilitating a workshop and a participant who was from Vietnam asked me what the word 'relentless' meant. He said that English was not his first language and he had never heard the word before.

While I could explain the definition, I struggled to think of a synonym on the spot. I didn't want to confuse the person with too many words, so I politely asked him whether he could use Google Translate – which he did. Once he saw the word, I asked what English word he would have used now knowing the Vietnamese alternative. He responded with 'nonstop', which I think is another awesome way to convey the meaning.

A relentless person is determined to do something and refuses to give up. Your role as a leader is to be relentless in the pursuit of a culture of service excellence. It takes lots of work and time, and when you achieve your goal, it doesn't stop there. Many leaders think that just because they give a message once it will stick or that being relentless will be seen as nagging or micromanaging.

While not discounting the achievements of organisations such as Disney, their budgets for lights, fireworks and dazzle do a lot to give the illusion of perfection, but behind the scenes the relentless approach to service runs through the veins of the organisation. Many organisations are not like Disney. You don't have the budgets nor are the lights and fireworks the thing you want to focus on. It requires more work from your entire leadership team to be relentless when it comes to service culture.

Relentless messaging is not about making your staff hear messages more than once, and it also doesn't suggest that they're not capable of hearing it the first time. Being relentless is not about what you're saying, but about the timing of when you say it. Sometimes we can be told something once with no impact, but when we hear it at the right time it can make a huge difference. It's hard to know the right time your staff member will be ready to hear your message, so by continuously having conversations means when the staff member is ready, you will be there with the message.

In the Introduction, I referred to the 1997 letter that Jeff Bezos wrote to the shareholders of Amazon in which he discussed the concept of high standards and whether they were intrinsic or teachable.[101] He believed you could learn high standards in any domain – in this case, customer service. To reach a high standard, he wrote that one must recognise what good looks like, and secondly have realistic expectations on how hard it will be to achieve that result.

Setting the standard or the goal is one thing, and we've outlined what that could be in Chapter 4 – to be renowned for a culture of service. We know what success looks like by everything in Chapters 5 through 9. The hardest part is setting the realistic expectations on how easy or difficult it will be. When it comes to a culture of service, it's usually harder than it first looks. This is why a leader must be relentless. Being relentless in pursuit of the desired standards will ensure you can push through over a long period of time and have the focus and attention required. Having customer-focused conversations is one of the most important parts of being a relentless leader.

QUESTION TO CONSIDER

- Is there a relentless approach to service messaging across the organisation?

13
Recognition

Celebrate service for repeat behaviours and wider adoption

People love celebrations, and a culture of service is something worth celebrating, but it needs the right kind of celebration. Leaders celebrate in the form of benefits, rewards and recognition. These three are grouped together, and a blurred line forms between them. It is important to see how each of the three celebrations differ.

A benefit is an added perk of working somewhere. Free parking and discounted services such as gym membership, health insurance and food are some of the main contenders. These are typically included for everyone who works for an organisation, so they don't need to do anything extra to earn them. This means that benefits don't work when it comes to service culture improvement.

A reward is something that is given to an employee or group of employees for completing a particular task or hitting a milestone. It usually has some form of monetary value or a slant toward something of leisure or recreation. Aside from a bonus, rewards are commonly found in competitions or internal campaigns among employees and can include movie tickets and grocery vouchers. Being rewarded with a $50 movie voucher for great customer service if you don't enjoy going to the movies is not much of a reward. If a monetary value does work for your teams though, you would be better off paying every single employee $50 a month to get them to serve better. It wouldn't be economical in the first instance and less prestigious. A reward is a 'dangling carrot' situation – with many limitations – which works best when incentivising staff to achieve targets well above a particular level.

Finally, we have recognition. Recognition is exactly what it says – being recognised for something. There may be a reward attached to it, there may not, but in its purest form the recognition itself is the accolade or commendation that counts. Recognition programs include 'employee of the month/quarter/year' where one or a group of employees are singled out for their achievements in a particular area.

Now that we've defined the three types of celebrations, it's important that these aren't confused when integrating them with a service culture program. As the chapter title suggests, recognition is the one to focus on.

The point of recognition is to encourage repeat behaviours and wider adoption of these behaviours across the entire team. When you look at the SECRET Service model you can see that it is on the right-hand team side, overlaid on the behaviour. A recognition program is the most appropriate way to bring out the behaviours we discussed in Chapter 8. Rewards have value, but the reward itself presents challenges.

Be aware too that customers can see through the organisations that are rewarding their staff for 'good customer service'. It's easy to notice when a staff member pressures you to fill out a survey because they know they will get something in return if you take the time to respond.

This chapter will unpack the core components of a great recognition program and how to steer clear of the many pitfalls that can detract from recognising customer service.

QUESTIONS TO CONSIDER

- What do we currently do in terms of benefits, rewards and recognition?
- Are they effective, and are there blurred lines between them?

Identify what customers value

The relationship between service behaviours and a recognition program is that they are both concrete in nature. There should be no ambiguity. If staff members are to be recognised for behaviours, they need to know what to do so it's not out of reach. When a person is recognised among their peers, other team members will want the same recognition opportunity and will try to emulate the behaviour.

When I ask a leader what their organisation does well in terms of service, the most common answer is they have friendly staff. While this may be true, the word 'friendly' is too ambiguous. When customers give feedback saying the staff are 'friendly', it's hard to know what specifically needs to happen to repeat it across the workforce. Everyone has their own version of what being friendly means. If one person is recognised for being friendly, the other would wonder why they didn't get recognised too. Therefore, the more ambiguous the program, the more it would be criticised, which limits its success.

The good news is that we've done the hard work for you already. We uncovered a list of behaviours in Chapter 8 that customers value and some examples of each one. Here's a quick recap. By treating a customer like a guest in your home, you can make them feel that:

- They **belong** in the organisation

- They are **comfortable**

- You're **prepared** for them

- You're **approachable**

- Things are **effortless**

- Things are **interesting**

- They will want to **return**

- You're **grateful** for them

- You're **genuine** to them

The reason we created nine behaviours was not to make service restrictive. We understand that every customer situation is different so the nine behaviours are not designed to be a process but a tool of behaviours that the staff can use when they see fit. When these behaviours are first introduced to your organisation, your program can recognise team member for times they've demonstrated one of them. By doing this in the early days, you are capturing real-life examples of how the behaviours specifically come to life. The more this is shared across your organisation, the more other staff members will learn what they can specifically do.

As we've discussed, different customers value different things. For instance, at a supermarket, a staff member who helps an elderly customer to their car with their shopping trolley is making things effortless, which would be appreciated. If they insist on carrying a customer's bag of groceries to their car when they don't need the help, they are making things effortless, but it's not valued by the customer. This is why porters at hotels ask whether you need help with your luggage, as sometimes you need it, other times you don't. The action is simply not enough here; it must be an action that the customer values linked back to the overarching behaviour.

QUESTIONS TO CONSIDER

- Do our staff know the signature service behaviours that are expected of them?
- Do our leaders demonstrate these behaviours in their interactions with staff members?

Setting realistic targets

I closed the end of the last chapter by talking about the relationship that being relentless has with realistic expectations. The setting of recognition targets must also be realistic.

In 2004, talk show host Oprah Winfrey kicked off her nineteenth season of television with the famous car giveaway, where every audience member was surprised with a brand-new car.[102] While there was a lot of hype, in business, everyone winning a recognition program is not the goal.

Let's say you are implementing a monthly recognition program for your service behaviours where you recognise one or two people. The point of the program is to encourage repeat behaviours and wider adoption, so while you are only recognising the top two performers, there should be many other people that are finalists or in the running. The prize of recognition shouldn't be 'scraping the barrel' for the only two people that were seen exhibiting the behaviours on the last day of the month. The competition for recognition should be between everyone who exhibited the behaviours in the last month, with the top one or two being the most impactful to both the customer and the organisation.

Realistic means that a large proportion of the staff should be hitting their behaviour targets while maintaining tension in terms of what they need to improve on. These people should be recognised in a 'pool' of finalists. If something is too out of reach, people will eventually stop trying to hit it, or their attention will soon shift to expect more of a 'reward' due to the additional effort they are putting in versus simply doing it for the recognition.

I have experienced organisations that meet as leaders and can't think of anyone who could be recognised for their service behaviours. It normally doesn't end well when they just pick someone randomly who immediately comes to mind or check who hasn't won yet. I have been a judge on many industry awards in the customer service category and, on occasions, the judges have agreed not to award a winner, only giving a highly commended award, because none of the submissions were worthy of the title. A recognition program should work in the same way. Make it realistic for everyone, but don't lower the standard if for some reason you don't have the quality examples you are looking for.

Using the behaviour examples from Chapter 8, we can further condense these into three core categories of behaviours that happen 1) early on in the interaction, 2) during the interaction and 3) later in the interaction.

The first three behaviours that happen early on (belong, comfortable and prepared) are all about the attentiveness of a person. When someone is attentive, they acknowledge a person to make them feel they belong. They recognise that someone is standing and ask them to take a seat. They anticipate a customer's needs. This is achieved by being attentive.

The second three behaviours that happen during the interaction (approachable, effortless and interested) are about how engaging a person is. When someone is engaging, they are open to an interaction and look for ways to make things easier for customers and add value to the interaction by sharing things that may interest them.

The final three behaviours that happen later in an interaction (want to return, grateful and genuine) are about how warm a person is. When someone is warm, they'll do something small that makes a real difference to the other person. They express thanks, appreciation or sorrow when things don't go a customer's way, and they sincerely farewell a customer when they finish serving them.

The opposites of these three core behaviours are examples of poor service and often commonly experienced by customers. For example, staff can be inattentive, unengaging, and cold. Therefore, it's useful to distinguish these apart from the desired behaviours so staff members know how they shouldn't behave and what won't count for recognition.

These three broader categories of early, during and later are still specific enough for staff members to keep in their mind at all times, without trying too hard to pick one of the specific nine behaviours. Once your team are grounded in the nine behaviours, the program could transition into focusing just on the three areas. You could even recognise a team member for each area to ensure that each one gets a spotlight every month. For example, a team member recognised for being attentive, one for being engaging and one for being warm.

You may offer an overall prize, like winning a career grand slam in tennis where someone joins the service hall of fame once they've been recognised for being attentive, engaging and warm. These three core behaviours are yet another example of something you could integrate in your conversations (discussed in Chapter 12) to keep this recognition program alive. The list of opportunities is huge, and you can implement a recognition structure that works for your organisation.

QUESTIONS TO CONSIDER

- If we started this program right now, would we have people in the organisation to recognise?
- How frequently are team members practising the desired behaviours?

Put the customer at the centre

If there's one part in this chapter to get right, it's this one. There are two ways to recognise staff. While neither is right or wrong, the first way is not the preferred one for service behaviours.

The first example is McDonald's, a global chain and well-oiled machine when it comes to many of their practices. Over the life of the organisation, they've figured out what works and doesn't work, and their testament to success is their longevity. Have you noticed that each staff member's name badge has up to four stars on it? Have you ever wondered what these four stars represent? Putting a star on a name badge is one way to recognise a person. They can proudly show a star for everyone to see – customers included. It goes without saying that the more stars the better.

This type of recognition system is one that recognises position not mission. In other words, the stars are based on the staff members' role within the organisation, and not the customer in any way. Each star represents four different modules of training: quality, service, cleanliness and operational excellence. As staff members are trained and competent in a different area of the restaurant, they achieve a star. When you see a staff member with four stars, as a customer you'll know they are competent in all the areas of restaurant operation like operating the till, preparing products, working in the dining areas, and hygiene and safety knowledge.

While this is not a criticism of the program, the question must be asked: what do any of the stars have to do with a customer? A customer wants to be reassured that the people serving them are trained and competent and would expect this. If a customer was served by a 'one-star' staff member, it wouldn't mean they weren't competent in their job – it just means they haven't completed all the training modules for the restaurant. Stars on name badges are assumed to be related to quality or excellence, but most customers don't explicitly know what the stars mean. The customers see the stars, but there's no information to what they mean unless they ask or look it up. In this example, the customer is not the centre of attention in the program.

The other way to recognise is to make the recognition relevant to the customers and let the customers know about it. This type of recognition is mission focused, not position focused. In other words, working in line with their purpose, not their position description.

Stars on name badges for this type of recognition is possible, but it can be done even more explicitly. Usually when someone is awarded 'staff member of the month', their recognition is kept to back of house areas. This misses a huge opportunity to communicate recognition to customers and engage them in how important they are to the business.

When my wife was in labour with our first child, I noticed in the foyer of the hospital an A3 sheet of paper in a plastic frame with 'staff member of the month' written on it, along with a photo of a bright, cheerful, smiling nurse with her name alongside it. It didn't include a description of what she had done to deserve this recognition. A detailed enough description outlining what the staff member did (their position), and how this relates or benefits their customers (their mission) would have been an interesting addition.

For example, let's say the reason she was awarded staff member of the month was because she stayed and completed a double shift when they were short staffed. This is absolutely a valid reason to recognise her, but most descriptions would end there. The description could be continued by saying '. . . as a result, our customer wait times that evening were kept well below our promise to triage every customer within fifteen minutes of arriving at the hospital.'

Business executive and author Seth Godin wrote in his blog about the simple truth of photo albums. He said when you give someone an album or a yearbook, the first thing they'll do is seek out their own picture.[103] Customers are the same. They don't want to walk through your organisation seeing internal marketing images of staff members unless there is a clear connection to how it's important to them. Like the old saying goes, 'If we had no customers, you wouldn't be here' – there's truth to that, so by incorporating customer service into a recognition program it demonstrates the importance of service to be more than just lip service.

QUESTIONS TO CONSIDER
- Do we let our customers know we recognise our staff?
- Can we make our recognition messaging more about the customer?

Everybody can recognise each other

One of the biggest problems with recognition programs is the lack of leadership presence on the frontline. By being more visible, they will be able to see and hear good news stories and be able to give recommendations for the recognition program.

As the old adage goes, 'There's never anyone around when I'm doing a good job, and there is always someone around when I'm not doing a good job.' Opportunities to shine do not always present themselves when the manager is around, so a recognition program needs to take this into consideration.

One of the side benefits of a recognition program is the extra camaraderie that exists between everyone in the organisation – including the ones who aren't recognised. If we give permission to the entire workforce to empower them to look for and be able to recognise one another's service behaviours, there will be more examples coming through to the leadership team to consider.

The rule of reciprocity works here – people are more than happy to recognise others, not because they expect a recognition in return, but because they know if others operate the same way, the same gesture of recognition may be repaid in the future. When this occurs, it ensures there is a pipeline full of recognised behaviours. It stops that old cliché of the manager stepping out from their office on the last day of the month with a clipboard and quickly 'assessing' the handful of staff that are on shift to have a recommendation ready for the managers' meeting the following morning.

This concept isn't hard to grasp at department level but should also work across the entire organisation. That means if the CEO or a head of another department notices a service behaviour being performed by someone in another team, they too have the power to recognise the behaviour. Healthy competition is great in business, but if leaders are too focused on their departments only, silos can begin to form and the big picture slips out of focus. One department that outperforms the rest will not on its own make the organisation renowned for their service excellence. Like the old saying goes, 'All boats benefit from a rising tide.'

When leaders recognise behaviours across departments and when these are formally posted to the entire organisation, the departments will learn from each other about how to deliver exceptional service. Sometimes it can seem challenging to figure out what to do with a customer situation until you see it done a different way somewhere else. The program will eventually become a knowledge repository of many behaviour examples that can be shared across the company, including in new staff inductions.

QUESTIONS TO CONSIDER

- Am I always on the lookout for great examples of service behaviours across the organisation?
- Do I give the organisation permission to recognise other departments?

14
Evaluation

Continuously improving service

When you look at the SECRET Service model, we're now at the point where the overlay on the CABS model doesn't sit in a particular section but on top of intersecting points. Sitting in the centre, evaluation is a highly important leadership practice that will help directly improve the service culture of the organisation. Evaluation is underrated and the sheer power of it is seldom used to its full potential.

I have been fortunate to have worked for a seasonal organisation full time but with a closed trading period in the winter. While seasonal businesses have their challenge of stopping and starting their trade, the closed period in the middle of the year forces the team to stop, reflect and aim to start the following season stronger than the season before.

I've also had the privilege of being an educator in the classroom. One of the signature parts of any training course is the feedback form at the end of a session. Teachers have reflective practice built into their job by way of feedback. My exposure to this has made reflection and continuous improvement a core part of everything I do.

You'll notice I've used the word feedback and evaluation a few times already in Part Three. These words are often used interchangeably, and it's worth clarifying the difference between them.

When an evaluation takes place, a judgement is formed on whether something is good or bad, effective or ineffective. Feedback, on the other hand, is a way to collect information which is then used to form an evaluation. For example, a workshop participant completes a feedback form not an evaluation form. They give feedback which is taken among other feedback to form an evaluation on the effectiveness of a lesson. Likewise, customers don't formally evaluate your organisation, they give feedback that helps you objectively make an evaluation.

This chapter will explore several processes and practices to make evaluation an integral part of your organisation, including ways to measure the improvements. Reflection on what your organisation currently does in terms of continuous improvement as evaluation is something that needs to be embraced by the entire leadership team if it is to be useful.

There's a number of reasons why a culture of evaluation doesn't come naturally to organisations. Lack of knowledge in terms of what to do with feedback is one thing, but mainly it is the fact that getting feedback exposes people and the organisation to negativity and criticisms especially if the feedback was unsolicited. Sometimes people aren't willing to see or admit their flaws, or they might take things personally. According to research by Gallup, 26% of employees say their performance is evaluated less than once a year, while 48% say they are reviewed annually.[104] It's safe to say that evaluation is not used to its full potential, and no wonder it's lacking when it comes to service.

The reality of feedback can also expose leaders who may not know what's going on in their business. You could argue that if a leader knows what's happening with their customers, no feedback should come as a surprise. The feedback can strengthen or confirm what is already known. This chapter will potentially highlight some of the not so positive things that exist in relation to your customer service culture.

In 2014, food and beverage company Honey Maid launched a campaign 'This is Wholesome', which featured blended families (families that were interracial, immigrants and families with same-sex parents). After the ads were released, they created another commercial that acknowledged the reactions the previous commercials had on the public. It explored how much negative feedback was received regarding their ads. It contrasted the negative feedback by exploring the positive messages they received – which numbered over ten times more than the negative messages.[105]

It was a powerful campaign that we can learn so much from. When it comes to evaluation, we are often consumed by the negative feedback or the criticisms and look past the positives that are out there too.

QUESTIONS TO CONSIDER

- Do you feel that customer feedback is taken seriously in your organisation?
- Overall, do you think there is more positive or negative feedback being received?
- Does feedback come as a surprise to you?

Measuring the effectiveness of service practices

As the old saying goes, 'What gets measured, gets managed.' Leaders and business are big on measurement and data.

If you've picked up this book, chosen to read it and got this far through, it's likely that you don't need any convincing about the value of service culture to an organisation's bottom line. There are many anecdotal sayings that if you take care of your people and customers, profit will follow, and broadly that is true. Research by Deloitte and Touche found that 60% of companies that were customer-centric were more profitable than companies who weren't.[106]

When a culture comes together, everybody within it wants to see a feeling of progress. However, there is a reason why measuring progress has been left so late in the book.

Reflect back on Chapter 4 when we explored the ladder from repulsed to renowned, and dysfunctional to exceptional. You'll note in the third column under business focus, the word 'measure' wasn't used until the level of a 'great' culture. We discussed that when a service culture is improved from a stereotypical needs-based level (below the line), the small incremental shifts in culture and focus are worth more than the measurement which can be assigned to it.

It doesn't mean if you're coming from a low base, you can't take measurements or collect data. It means that if you make measurements and data your core focus, the results will seem low, and the growth will be slow. There may be incremental moves worth noting, but it's worth more to focus on the bigger picture than the specific measurements.

This is like when you are dieting for weight loss. You can weigh yourself twice a day, but you may not notice much of a difference. If you eat healthily, exercise and sleep better, you will get into a routine that makes you feel better first, focusing on the numbers on the scale later.

Now that we're officially looking at measurement, the biggest issue is knowing what to measure. This is difficult as, in the people and culture area, there are many variables that contribute to something working or not. You might have one thing right, but something else is bringing down your results, so by mistake you stop doing what's right.

Profit is a great example. Focusing only on profit could suggest your service culture practices aren't working if profit isn't increasing. The reality is your service culture practices may be working well, but there are some other things in the business such as sale price, loss or high operating expenses that are contributing to the hit in profit.

Another thing to mention here is that all the data you measure is lagging in nature, so you should try to figure out how to incorporate real-time data in your organisation as well. Think about being a rideshare passenger for Uber. From the comfort of your own phone at the time of the trip, you can give feedback, rate the driver and customise your journey. This may not be possible depending on your industry, but don't rule it out. Keep looking for ways to measure real-time feedback.

Despite talking about lagging indicators of data, the process of evaluation is one which is continuous in nature. It's not done once at a point in time and once only. While people like to collect immediate data and see immediate progress, the journey of measurement should be looked at over a long-term period.

Since Chapter 10, the SECRET Service model has explored several leadership practices that align with both the employee life cycle and the employee experience. To measure the effectiveness of each of these would be a good place to start given the considerable effort placed on them.

Correlate these metrics with what you have read in the previous chapters of Part Three of this book:

- **Selection**: Measure the hiring ratio as well as unsolicited resumes handed in to the organisation or enquiries for job opportunities.

- **Education**: Collect training feedback after each session.

- **Conversation**: Collect the number of suggestions/ideas and frequency of conversations.

- **Recognition**: Measure the number of people recognised, and good news stories received.

- **Evaluation**: Count the number of customer referrals. Collect customer feedback and review site ratings (more in this chapter).

- **Tradition**: Record staff attrition/absenteeism/engagement.

QUESTIONS TO CONSIDER

- Are we using some of the metrics above to measure our service culture?
- Are there others you could add that you're already using?

A process for actioning customer feedback

Psychologist Adam Grant said, 'Requesting feedback doesn't signal insecurity. It demonstrates that you care more about your learning than your ego.'[107] By now you should be open to requesting that feedback from your customers, if you are not doing so already.

Once the feedback comes to your organisation, what do you literally do with it? I mean literally – whether it's an email, a handwritten letter or typed on a review site, what do you do with the feedback? Creating a defined process for dealing with customer feedback demonstrates that you're not just going through the motions of collecting it but that you take it seriously.

Whether you formally collect feedback or not, it's fair to say that there is feedback out there. The more an organisation embraces it, the greater the chance of improvements in their service culture. The world-class service-driven organisations are service driven because of their evaluation processes. Some feedback has merit for consideration, other feedback not as much. For now, let's assume any feedback you receive has a mountain of gold beneath it.

Before we look at what to do with the feedback, we should first explore what can be done to increase the quality of the feedback received. There are a range of ways to collect feedback. Online forms, paper forms, direct emails, direct phone calls, focus groups – the list goes on. Every avenue of feedback has its own merits and not one is better than the other. The most important part of collecting feedback is to make sure that customers feel comfortable to give it, and not pressured.

In 2019, I visited Albany in the Great Southern Region of Western Australia. Among other things, Albany is known as the location where 41,000 troops left Australia to battle in World War I. As a tribute to the centenary of the war, a temporary art installation of 16,000 flower-like shining spheres was installed. This moving and solemn place was called the Field of Light – Avenue of Honour. What struck me was what was written on the feedback card I collected as I left: 'Perhaps there are no words at the moment, but once you've had a chance to process how the Field of Light – Avenue of Honour made you feel, please tell us.' This was such a befitting sentence for such a place. Far better than if a person stood at the exit and ambushed me to find out whether I enjoyed my experience. Notice the focus was also on how it made me feel, and not 'what I liked' about it.

The second part of collecting customer feedback is in the wording of what you are asking for. In 2018, a brand-new 60,000-seat sports stadium was opened in Perth. There was much debate in the beginning over the type of food served, with criticism that not enough healthy food options were available. When asking for customer feedback about stadium food, there are two ways to do this, both of which would yield different answers.

- **Question One**: Do you think there should be more healthy food options at Perth Stadium? (Most people would say yes.)

- **Question Two**: What sort of food would you most likely purchase when attending a sport event at Perth Stadium? (Most people would say junk food.)

Both responses are valid, but the fact that two questions give two different answers about the same topic means we need to be more vigilant in terms of how we are wording our feedback questions. If we don't, the actions resulting from feedback could send the organisation in the wrong direction.

The final aspect is to assess whether collecting feedback is required. Sometimes organisations ask for feedback for almost every step or stage in a process. Parcel delivery services often come under scrutiny, especially on Twitter, when customers receive links asking for feedback of their service. Some tweets contain something like the following rant: 'You delivered my package. That was your job. Well done. What more do you need to know?'

I'm not saying the postal service can't ask for feedback, but you must question how asking for feedback may look from a customer's perspective – remember we want to reduce customer effort, not add to it. We touched on this earlier, but something hard to accept is that the bulk of feedback you receive will not be from people who have had a good experience.

The next step is the process for what to do with feedback. Assuming you've asked the right questions at the right time, your customers will give you a mountain of gold to work with. There are four specific things we can do with every piece of feedback. These are not designed to create work, but to put the feedback through a process which captures as much of the value as possible which may not be obvious at first glance. You need to ensure the value doesn't get buried.

1. Listen to customers

Customers who take the time to give feedback want to be heard. If they think this won't happen, they are more likely to ignore your request. Communicate to the customer that their feedback has been received and read verbatim to the staff or summarised if it was negative. Doing this gives the customer confidence that something has been done with it. Just doing this first step is more than most organisations do and when someone takes the time to give feedback, the acknowledgement is powerful.

2. Insights from customers

Examine the feedback beyond the words and see if you can gain some further insights about what the customer is asking for, what's important to them and how it has made them feel. As you do this, you are gaining additional data that may help with responding to the feedback, and how you modify systems or processes that might be causing the negative feedback. You could use the feedback to monitor whether other customers feel the same way. You may not necessarily agree, but if you approach feedback with an open mind then you may learn something from your customers.

3. **Improvements with customers**

Make the feedback two-way. This may not be required for every bit of feedback, and the customer might not want to engage with you further, which you need to respect. We briefly discussed the concept of curiosity in Chapter 9, and there's no more perfect time to be curious than when you've received constructive feedback. While the feedback is fresh, you could contact the customer and gain a deeper understanding of the problem, even sense-checking whether the customer is satisfied with the remedy or the response, or whether they could give you any further information. This is an ideal time to ask customers whether they would or wouldn't value a particular type of service. You may have in your mind what good service is, but if the customer doesn't value it, it may not be worth implementing throughout your team.

4. **Planning for customers**

Feedback doesn't always come in at the most convenient time. While the feedback can have merit, it could be something that isn't a priority for now or is a planned priority for the future. For example, customers of shopping centres may complain that the toilets are too far to walk to. It may not be economical to simply build new toilets then, but the centre might be waiting for a redevelopment to take place in a year or two.

It would be a complete oversight if the plans for the redevelopment were drawn up without listening to the feedback received historically. There should be a file of customer feedback for future planning that should be accessed whenever a major project occurs.

These four steps are a good tool to sense-check how much merit feedback has. Sometimes feedback contains no information (or no useful information) or is clearly not genuine. You have absolute control to look at feedback and assess any merits of what you read and what is asked of you and your organisation. Don't listen to customers because I said so, but don't ignore them either because you think they're wrong. That's why making the evaluation separate from the feedback will ensure the right decision has been made.

If you're at this point and are struggling with a lack of feedback, there is one creative way to get some. In Chapter 1, we explored how it's important to try and get feedback early and in person and not to push customers to become keyboard warriors. The Ovolo Hotel group have been creative in that regard. I saw a sign in one of their hotels once that said, 'Got feedback? Tell the CEO yourself! ceo@ovologroup.com We will respond!' Telling your customers that their feedback goes directly to the CEO might just be the way to get more of it.

QUESTIONS TO CONSIDER

- Do you have a process in place to deal with customer feedback?
- Could you allocate a resource for this to take place?

Effectively responding to feedback online

This is not a chapter on social media – it's one on evalua-tion – but it would be remiss of me not to include a section on one of the biggest ways feedback can be captured in business today. Social media began as a tool to communi-cate and stay in contact with one another. Research suggests that 91.9% of marketing departments in companies with over 100 staff members were expected to use social media for their marketing.[108] More specifically, social media pages and review sites are actively used by organisations to reach more customers more often and collect feedback more immediately as people can now communicate at the touch of a personal smartphone.

The world of online feedback is also contentious. Any #CustomerServiceFail can soon go viral, be mocked by light-hearted news programs and create a buzz of opinions around the office. Even an Australian comedy series *Rostered On* focuses on the daily customer service struggles of retail staff. People love talking about bad service. There are many times I've been interviewed in the media or on a podcast where the conversation has quickly turned into listening to people's frustrations about customer service.

Rajashri Srinivasan, a business professor at the University of Texas, identified that the trend of online com-plaints started after a 2009 incident went viral.[109] It unfolded when Canadian musician Dave Carroll wrote a song titled 'United Breaks Guitars' and posted it on YouTube after United Airlines broke his guitar during a flight.[110] Despite his numerous attempts to complain, the airline did not take him seriously and, as a result, he wrote a song to get the air-line's attention. At the time of writing this book, the video had over 22 million views.

Social media can bring out the humorous side of service too. I once read a tweet from an organisation that said, 'Thank you for buying our product. Please take a moment to give our competitors a one-star review.' Another, on a sign outside a café read, 'Come in and try the worst coffee one woman on TripAdvisor had in her life.'[111]

The world of online feedback and keyboard warriors can show the worst of customers, but it can also incite the worst from businesses. For the rest of this section, I will explore twenty points that are useful to consider if your organisation receives feedback from customers on social media or review sites.

1. Publicly respond to all positive feedback. This shows customers you value it, and it encourages them to do it again as they have been acknowledged.

2. Publicly respond to all negative feedback because it signifies to other customers who may read it that you have attended to it, and they can expect the issue to be resolved. People want to know they'll be looked after if things go wrong. Don't let the opposing extremes and varying opinions push you away from your values or core beliefs to the point that you become completely neutral in your responses. Make the decision when a response isn't required.

3. Respond early and regularly. Show customers that you have a habit of frequently checking feedback. How do you feel when you look at a review site that hasn't had any responses for five years? Show customers there is life on the other side of the keyboard. Are there people in your organisation that are trained and empowered to do this? Letting only one person do it could create a backlog and be less empowering to the team. It's useful to consider responding to feedback with the same urgency as you would to a new business enquiry.

4. Treat customers online or via email as you would face-to-face. Resist the temptation to lash back at any complaint. Businesses that have done this usually end up receiving criticisms for their responses.

5. Don't be overly concerned about other customers seeing, hearing or reading the negative complaint. Most people can spot the 'serial' complainer. Having said that, you should still be cautious about potential or new customers being exposed to negative reviews especially if it's their first impression of your brand.

6. Most complaints and compliments are service related. Pay attention to notice how often the product is complained about compared to the service.

7. Use any opportunity when you respond to negative feedback to demonstrate publicly your level of service. Exceptional service is typically seen when things go wrong, so take this opportunity and use it to its full potential.

8. Be careful how you ask for further feedback or what you tell your customer to do online. Remember things should be easy for them, so try not to give them tasks or put any expectations on them.

9. Never rig or skew review sites or feedback. Transparency is key, and if something gets heated, do not disable the site. There have been occasions where organisations have lashed back at customers and then taken their own review site down, which doesn't look good, especially if the media have taken screenshots. In 2019, airline Garuda Indonesia came under fire for trying to block people (in this case an aviation blogger) from documenting their on-board experience.[112] In 2016,

Meriton Serviced Apartments were taken to the Federal Court in Australia for stopping customers with negative experiences from being reminded to give a review on TripAdvisor.[113]

10. Understand the customer's real motive for complaining. Is it to inflict as much damage as possible? Ask yourself why you found out about it online first? Was there an opportunity to receive it in person?

11. Avoid euphemisms, jargon and scripted responses. The customer took the time to write to you, so make sure you respond with heart. This includes signing off with your name and position and not simply writing 'Management'.

12. Try to make private and offline contact with the customers as well. Don't be offended if they don't want to talk to you, but always offer. The review sites are not a place for a full interaction or exchange between the customer and your organisation.

13. Explain to the customer what you will do with their feedback.

14. Actively read your own review sites (regardless of level in the organisation). You should have a good hand on what people are saying about your organisation. While you're at it, have a look at your competitors' review sites, as there could be some opportunities for improvement that you haven't considered. Depending on the number of reviews, it might be overwhelming to go through all of them, so a good rule of thumb that is useful for condensing information is to focus on the three-star reviews. If you adopt the mindset that the five-star reviews are by friends and family and

the one-star reviews are from the serial complainers (which may not be accurate but is a helpful stance to take), the three-star reviews may be more constructive in nature, leaving you much more aware of where you can improve. It's not a science, but something worth considering.

15. If a customer contacts you to complain, never send them away to complain in writing. It doesn't mean you should scare customers away from using social media as this can also be a brilliant marketing tool for the organisation. Just make sure you make it easy to complain in person if possible.

16. Investigate all 'truths'. In 2017, a plumbing business in Perth, Western Australia sent a customer a 'cease and desist' letter claiming an online review was untrue and defamatory.[114] While you shouldn't tolerate defamation, if someone said they waited two hours but it was really fifteen minutes, investigate why it felt so long (ie standing in the hot sun etc. . .). Keep in mind that customers often use smartphones to capture things, including recording interactions with staff members. This creates evidence that should be considered.

17. Better service on social media means that frontline staff are wasted. If customers know that they can get a response from your social media team quicker than if they spoke to a real human, you are missing an opportunity to deal with feedback in person. It's good to give customers options for how to complain but you should never forget in-person feedback. It's a serious issue if an algorithm on a chatbot can detect a customer's emotions through language but a human cannot do the same through empathy.

18. If the complaint is false, try to agree on the message behind the complaint, not the specific detail. For instance, at a shopping centre a customer might complain that there are not enough disabled parking spaces. Legally there might be more than enough, but your response should not be to correct the customer, it should be about the message behind the complaint. In this case, the customer values accessibility. Make your response about shopping centre access and how you value it too.

19. Try to see how you can get real-time feedback and not just retrospective or lagging feedback. Spending some time on the frontline observing is one way to do it. If you opt for a tablet with a red, orange and green smiley face for real-time feedback, make sure the wording is specific, so the customer knows exactly what they are rating.

20. Examine your data. One five-star review versus 200 four-star reviews – what does it tell you? Are your customers giving enough feedback? Is there an overall increase or decrease in customer complaints year-on-year? One bad review should be taken seriously, although overall, it may not be statistically significant – in other words it is not representative of how the majority of customers may be feeling.

These twenty 'commandments' are a fabulous tool for training staff who respond to customer complaints. There may be exceptions to the rule depending on the nature and severity of a complaint, where I'm sure you would seek more specific advice on what to do. These are designed for customer complaints in general nature and not for full scale crisis or public relations disasters.

QUESTIONS TO CONSIDER

- Do we empower or give permission to our staff to respond to customer feedback directly (not just on social media)?
- Do you find yourself worried about what customers might say or write online?
- Do you actively contribute positive reviews to other review sites of businesses that you are a customer of? (The rule of reciprocity may apply here. Taking the time to help other businesses demonstrates your ability to 'give' instead of always wanting to receive feedback.)
- Are you confident that what you promise your customers will be delivered?

Walking in the customer's shoes

Much of this chapter has been spent looking at evaluation and feedback on paper, spreadsheets and online. The last part of this chapter is to look at another tool for evaluation that can be done in person.

Many organisations are familiar with mystery shopping, and they are quick to select this as a way to gather feedback. At the beginning of this chapter, I discussed how the more connected a leader is to the customer-facing roles in the organisation, the less feedback will present itself as a surprise.

For organisations that have a strong presence on the frontline, mystery shopping usually tells them what they already know. Or in some cases, it can give inaccurate information because it is a prescriptive checklist that doesn't take into account real-life circumstances that may affect this. For example, a mystery shopping report may say, 'Did not answer the phone within three rings', but doesn't provide any context about the factors that may have contributed to this.

Mystery shopping done well is used to measure service behaviours, such as those discussed in Chapter 8, and contributes to a recognition program as discussed in Chapter 13. A great starting template is to literally ask 'did the staff member. . .' contribute to the nine feelings in Chapter 8. For example, 'Did the staff member make you feel that you belong here?' and 'Did the staff member make you feel comfortable while serving you?' and so on.

Mystery shopping is a great tool if it can be connected to a tangible outcome that adds value to the business. It should not be used as something to scare staff into performing because they might be 'caught out' or confirm suspicions that the staff don't work well when you're not around. The premise of mystery shoppers is useful, but defaulting to a mystery shopper overlooks something right in front of the nose of leaders – their own staff, or even themselves.

Your staff members can't 'mystery' shop your organisation, but they can do what's known as 'walking in the customer's shoes'. A few times in this book we have talked about leaders such as Walt Disney and Richard Branson, who have been notably connected to the realities on the frontline. There's even the story of the school principal who stands outside their school to greet students every morning. There is a case for leaders to be connected to the frontline, but this can be taken further.

A leader on the frontline is only looking at things through the eyes of a leader and not a customer. They can try to wear both hats, but they're not fully experiencing things from the customer's perspective as a real customer. A program for walking in the customer's shoes does just that. It encourages leaders to take time off work and be a customer for a day and see what it's like for them when they use your business. If you have multiple sites, it's a good idea for them to try different sites to help freshen up the process.

It's a straightforward process, but there are a couple of pitfalls to look out for. A few years ago, I was assisting in implementing a 'walking in the customer's shoes' program for a water theme park. If there's any place you'd like to be in the customer's shoes, it would be a theme park. We piloted the program by asking a leader to spend a day in the water park and collect some thoughts on the customer service and the experience in general. There were no other instructions given.

When we reviewed how the leader spent the day, we found out the following. The leader parked in the staff car park, entered through the staff entry, put their belongings in their office (not in the lockers), wore shoes the whole day, carried a water bottle all day and popped into the office once or twice. This wasn't the fault of the leader but lack of clarity in the program.

We amended the program to contain a few conditions. Park your car in the customer car park and queue up at the customer entry. Use your own credit card to enter the park (we'll reimburse you later). Decide what to do with your belongings, but only put them where customers can put them. Like most customers do, walk by the water slides with bare feet and leave your water bottle with your belongings.

This was not designed to punish or make the experience difficult. It was designed to make the leader do what a typical customer would do. Customers who came off a waterslide but went onto another ride did not have shoes on and they would complain how the hot ground made it uncomfortable to walk on. Customers who needed water found it an effort to walk to the nearest kiosk. Some customers returned to their car to find it had been broken into.

No leader's car was broken into during this program, but that's not the point. The point is to make sure that leaders can experience things from the customer's perspective so they can relate to things that customers raise, as well as spend time thinking about the following few points:

- How are you noticing others being served around you, not just yourself?

- What do you overhear customers saying?

- How do you feel at certain times?

- Was anything memorable that you would previously think of as underrated?

- Was anything disappointing that you would previously think of as memorable?

- If you brought your family, how did you enjoy your time with them?

- How did it feel using your own money? Did it represent value?

- Did you notice any back of house things that detracted from the overall experience?

While experiencing the organisation from the customer's per-spective, the leader can look at the areas that were lacking and imagine new ideas or different ways of doing things. Often these could be quick and easy ideas that can be implemented straight away, leading to immediate service improvements. Longer term ideas can be logged for future planning for when the time is right.

These programs don't just work at theme parks, but in many front-facing customer environments as well. It doesn't have to be for a day; it could be for a few hours. It could also involve calling the main switchboard to see how your call is answered or dealt with, or even using the app, navigating the website or making an online purchase.

Walking in the customer's shoes is about shifting from subjective to objective, inward-facing to outward-facing, being too close to looking from a distance, working in the business to working on the business. It doesn't have to be a core focus, but something done annually by each leader at different times can be valuable when you are comparing this experience along with the other feedback you review as part of the evaluation process. To clarify, this is in addition to leaders spending time working on the frontline for a day every 2.5 months as introduced in Chapter 7.

QUESTIONS TO CONSIDER

- Have you thought about what it would be like to experience your organisation from a customer's perspective?
- Do you see a 'walking in the customer's shoes' program like this working in your organisation?

15
Tradition

Treating colleagues as internal customers

You've reached the last chapter of the book, and as the saying goes, 'last but certainly not least'. There's a reason why tradition has been left until the end. When you look at the SECRET Service model, it's the glue that brings everything together.

In the Introduction we explored one of the disconnects between leaders and human resource teams, but it's not only these two departments that can clash. Entire organisations can be built on silos that have developed over long periods of time, which can stifle the best efforts to make improvements to service cultures. A sure sign that the culture internally is not where it should be is if you hear gossip around how staff are expected to take care of customers, but no one takes care of them.

As Richard Branson said, 'If you take care of your employees, they'll take care of your customers.'[115] But for many there seems to be this disconnect between the way we treat external customers and the way we treat internal customers. I've even been a participant in a customer service training program that has spent the opening minutes clarifying the difference between these two.

While there are subtle differences between internal and external customers, it's not helpful to make the distinction. Why? There's no real difference between them anyway, and no real difference in how they should be treated. They are people and customers to someone. If your organisation works in business-to-business, or wants to work on internal culture, then everything in this book is still applicable. The more we start making distinctions and different rules for external customers, the more we treat internal customers differently. You may not call your colleagues 'customers', but regardless of what you call them, they should be treated as customers.

You can even take this further and think about the difference between customers, and those loved ones in your family. The concept of the relationship and what makes a great relationship is the same. Sure, there is a degree of intimacy at home that customers don't experience, and a degree of formality with customers that your family don't experience, but the concept of relationships are, in essence the same.

In Part Two when we looked at the CABS model, I introduced things that we already do that can be brought into the workplace. As humans we are already wired to be of service to one another, but we need that little bit of help to make sure it doesn't fall apart at work.

I've discussed how people mistakenly focus service efforts on the frontline departments because they are the most obvious and frequent customer touchpoint. This is where most of the quick wins are but investing in service and culture here can hurt more when they realise the expectation of external service is different to the internal service they receive. Leaders sometimes think that fixing the frontline will make everything better, but it doesn't work that way. It's like taking a fresh driving course as an adult and watching someone else break the rules of the road. It's more noticeable and irksome because you're doing the right thing and others aren't.

A GP office once called me in to discuss some service education for the reception team. While I was waiting in the reception to meet the owner of the practice (who was a doctor), I observed one of the doctors throw a file onto the desk next to the receptionist. He didn't throw it at her, but he threw it at the desk, and as he walked away said, 'File that one away.'

He probably didn't mean any malice behind it, but certain industries can shift power between frontline workers and others in the business. For the receptionist, the same care that we talk about in this book wasn't given to her. How would she be able to be of service to a customer after experiencing that?

Applying the learnings from this book to the way we treat our team internally is the best way to start. Reflect on the nine behaviours we explored in Chapter 8. Do you make your staff feel that they belong? Do you make them feel comfortable? Continue down the list.

QUESTIONS TO CONSIDER

- What is the internal culture like in your organisation?
- Are there silos between teams and/or departments?

Everyone relies on someone for service

Who do you serve? Someone must rely on you to get their job done. Who serves you? You must rely on someone for you to get your job done.

Your entire organisation is made up of people who serve one another. As we discussed earlier in the book, functional service is different to being of service. People may get the job done but are they being of service when they work?

The biggest misconception when it comes to internal customer service is that the customers externally are insulated from everything that goes on inside the workplace. I've heard stories where people say, 'Everyone fights with each other internally, but we do a great job at making sure our customers don't notice', like it's an achievement to be proud of. It is true that you can try to insulate external customers from the things that go on internally. Those traits of tactfulness, diplomacy and professionalism can help in this instance, but the insulation is not leak-proof.

Anytime there is a service failure on the frontline it can be traced to something happening internally. Think of problems internally like skeletons in the wardrobe – they'll find a way out. The same applies with you and your team personally. If they have things going on in their personal lives, they may try to suppress them, but, ultimately, they will affect their work. Equally, it's true about the things that go on internally between colleagues and how they affect customers externally.

Here's an example. One of the colleagues in a department gets an email about a product that's out of stock due to delays in shipping. The manager tells the colleague to go to the other staff on the shop floor and make sure they're aware of the stock issue and what to tell customers. This colleague doesn't get on with one of the other staff members. They don't fight, but each believes that the other doesn't pull their weight.

Therefore, this member of staff decides not to share this information with their colleagues on the floor and leaves for the day. The staff member on the floor is approached by a customer who is enquiring about the product that's out of stock. The staff member is less helpful because they don't know about the stock issue or when the shipment will be due in. The customer isn't angry but leaves without being helped – and as we discussed in Chapter 6, pleasant service that is not helpful is not being of service.

Not sharing information in this case was a deliberate act, but there could be many similar acts that go on like this every day unconsciously. Usually, they are to do with communication, power struggles or silos between departments which have formed, often due to stereotypes that exist about each other.

My wife and I were once shopping for baby monitors, and the staff member helping us apologised that she wasn't familiar with all of the technical elements of each product. As she was busy with us, she turned to a nearby colleague and asked her if she could call someone more experienced to assist. The colleague abruptly called back 'call her yourself'. This is a prime example where broken service internally is not only visible to the customer, but ultimately made an impression on us, the customers. Whatever the reason was that the staff member responded in that way was simply not appropriate.

Other common clashes include people who don't call the IT helpdesk and waste time trying to fix things themselves because they are afraid they will be belittled for not being tech savvy and confused when the technician uses jargon. The IT department never seems to get the sense of urgency, and they never leave the desk and chairs as they found them after fixing the computer. Could the IT department be of better service to their customers? Of course. I'm not suggesting this happens with every IT department, but the stereotype is there. As we explored in Chapter 4 about flipping the stereo-type externally, we must also flip the stereotype internally too.

Improving the internal service within the organisation is all about rapport. Rapport is the close and harmoni-ous relationship between people where they understand each other's feelings, respect ideas and communicate well together. Some people say rapport is about being on the same page, others say it's about being in sync with the other person. People regrettably mistake being in rapport for being forced to like another person. One of the easiest ways to build rapport is to find common ground and learn about each other's interests.

I'm not a fan of cricket so I love the cricket analogy. Someone who hates watching cricket is not in rapport with a colleague who absolutely loves cricket. They don't even know what an 'innings' or 'over' is. The non-cricket fan goes up to the cricket fan begrudgingly and reluctantly tries to build rapport. Nothing happens, and they give up, miss-ing the point that building rapport is not about the topic of cricket, it's about the other person. Wanting to learn more about another person so you can work together is what cre-ates rapport, not forcing yourself to like a sport.

Your staff will be building rapport with their customers every single day. They don't force themselves to like a sport or an interest; they focus on the person and build the relation-ship around the person. Engaging with a customer's interest or hobby is an avenue to build rapport. The same rule could be applied to colleagues internally. Yet, this doesn't always happen. This isn't a book on team building, but if we can take the way we build relationships with customers and apply the same to colleagues, there will be a lot more rapport and less skeletons in the wardrobe that make their way out to the frontline. Something as simple as this could be the reason why service on the frontline isn't where it should be.

QUESTIONS TO CONSIDER

- Are external customers treated differently to internal customers?

- Do staff try to insulate external customers from what goes on behind closed doors?

- Are there departments that conform to a negative stereotype that makes working with them more difficult?

- Is there an organisational structure of the working relationships between departments in your organisation?

Creating a supportive environment

Over the last few chapters, we've explored the different touchpoints where leaders can influence service culture. Firstly, there has been an implication that the leaders will work together. Secondly, they will lead by example in the way they treat all the staff.

If there is one common silo that forms, it is usually between front of house and back of house teams, or between staff on the frontline and their leaders (who are sometimes considered to be back of house).

I was once asked to come in and observe a large organisation run their group interview – known as an assessment centre. It took most of the day and was an opportunity for the prospective staff to get a glimpse into the company, and for the organisation to run a series of exercises to assess suitability for employment. My role was to observe and provide feedback on ways they could improve it.

At the beginning, one of the heads of recruitment stood up and said, 'We're like a family here.' It was a long room, so I turned to the other end where there was a row of managers leaning on the wall and on their mobile phones. Sometimes people say we're like a family, but their actions don't necessarily demonstrate it.

In this instance, the assessment centre was created by the HR team to improve on culture fit and retention of the right people, but it was not supported by the other leaders who would have benefitted from the time and investment in the assessment centre.

Chapters 10 through 13 covered four specific activities or touchpoints that are required to bring together a culture of service: selection, education, conversation and recognition. When I see an organisation for the first time, my best indicator of culture is how involved everyone gets in these four areas. I'm often not surprised, but I rarely see an organisation where everyone is involved in selection. An organisation where all the leaders turn up to welcome people at induction, where non-customer-facing teams have customer-related conversations and people who don't have direct reports not getting involved in recognition programs. Many organisations think that non-operational leaders without large teams (like finance or IT) don't need to attend inductions. By having those leaders present they are not only able to show support in welcoming the new staff but the new staff can put a face to a name for someone they may not interact with very often.

People are busy but should never be too busy for culture. These four activities at the minimum must have support from everyone on the leadership team. The portfolios of selection, education, conversation and recognition should be shared by the entire organisation regardless of who is in charge on the organisational chart.

Leaders can push back too. If a leader of a business doesn't have time to attend an induction (even if it's on a roster among other leaders and only for the first fifteen minutes to welcome everyone), they are clearly caught up in other activities that are not contributing any value to the culture of service. I know a large training organisation that has their leaders on a rotating roster to help greet and register participants who arrive for training every morning, which is another example of ensuring a customer focus is built into leaders' calendars.

The diary of a leader should be treated the same way as every other member of the organisation. Refer to Chapter 7 on attitudes and ensure that if your leaders refuse to participate in core service culture events, you can remove or reassign the things that are keeping them busy at this time. The right leader will make the time, but calendars do get the better of people every now and then. Sometimes a leader can start off being supportive, but they slowly get out of participating in these key activities. That's why it's a good idea to keep on top of it.

The other part of leadership support is the ability of leaders to serve on the frontline. An unknown author said, 'If serving is below you, leadership is beyond you.' This speaks true to the reluctance of leaders helping out from time to time.

There will always be opportunities for anyone, including leaders, to lend a hand from time to time. A great example is when a receptionist is serving a customer in person and the phones are ringing off the hook. I've seen organisations that have an overflow function where if the receptionist can't get to the call, it moves on to other people in the office to answer it. Another example is a supermarket that automatically opens a checkout when a queue has more than two people waiting, or an airport worker checking in business class passengers calls for customers from the economy line if they don't have anyone waiting in their queue. It may seem like an inconvenience, but those organisations that automatically help a customer in ad hoc situations are really demonstrating just how service focused they are.

Calling on a leader from another department to jump on the cash register due to short staffing isn't a long-term solution. I'm talking about the times that hit crisis mode. Unforeseeable times that need everyone to rally together for their customers.

I once worked for an airline as a check-in agent. One day there was a nationwide system outage for the check-in system. Planes were grounded and customers who were arriving at the airport had nowhere to wait but in the terminal with the queue snaking outside into the car park.

At this time, the airline had staff members from the city office come to the airport and help out. As the computer system wasn't working, they were helping in more manual ways including being present to direct and reassure customers. This is a brilliant example of business continuity planning (BCP), but, in essence, the principle is about service. It's OK to be transparent about issues or staffing shortages, but it is not an excuse for not pulling out all the stops to ensure people are there to serve customers in a crisis.

The more we expose leaders to the way the frontline works, the more useful they will be in situations like these. As we discussed earlier, everyone who works at Zappos must start by spending two weeks in the call centre. Two weeks may or may not be overkill for your organisation, but consider exploring how much your leaders know about the operation of cash registers and check-in systems on the frontline. This would be learned if leaders spent a day every few months working on the frontline serving customers, as discussed in Chapter 7.

The final element of support and buy-in is usually lacking from those people who work in back of house departments in roles such as the kitchen staff, the people loading bags onto planes and the mechanics of theme park rides. The back of house team plays an integral role in organisations and some people prefer to work there. There's nothing wrong with this, and back of house roles shouldn't be forced to work on the frontline. However, just because someone works back of house doesn't mean they can't be exposed to the difference they make on the frontline.

A ride mechanic at a theme park doesn't see the joy on children's faces when they are on the rides. A kitchen hand doesn't see people enjoying their meals. A baggage handler doesn't see loved ones reunite at the airport. When a person works in a back of house role, they can quickly become disconnected to the difference they make and the purpose they are here to serve. From time to time, bring someone from back of house out to the frontline and show them the difference they make. Let them see the emotion on customers' faces and let them be proud of what they do to contribute to this.

It's not just about connecting them to the end outcome. There are many departments who have no idea what other departments do. They may view other teams as lazy or bottlenecking progress because they don't understand how everyone fits into the organisation. Taxi drivers spending time in the call centre is a great way to illustrate how learning what another department does can increase working relationships and understanding of the challenging circumstances they face each day. While I did say you should never force a back of house person to work on the frontline, as a minimum the people in these roles should be prepared for what they should say or do if they encounter a customer.

A friend of mine once told me about an experience she had at the Westin Hotel in Bali. Her son who was about six years old at the time approached one of the gardeners to ask for something. Not all the back of house team spoke English, but the gardener dropped his tools, listened to her son and called on a porter who was passing to assist the child.

Preparing your back of house teams for situations like this stops them from powerwalking in company uniform past customers who need help. A good mantra to adopt is to always acknowledge customers; otherwise, it looks like you're ignoring them. While customers may not expect someone in another department to solve their problem, the staff member can be helpful in finding someone who can help. In most cases, customers don't care who serves them as long as someone does. You need to be confident that none of your staff responds to customers by saying, 'I work back of house, you'll need to ask someone else.'

Cleaners at the Disneyland theme park are taught to draw the face of Mickey Mouse using their mop and bucket of water. This small gesture can sometimes be a highlight of a child's day and shows customers that the cleaning department are just as much part of the team as everyone else.

QUESTIONS TO CONSIDER

- Do you expect your leaders to be present at key culture-building events (like selection and education)?
- How well do different departments know what each other does?
- Do you have a business continuity planning system in place for leaders to help out on the frontline when there are unforeseen events?
- Could you start showing back of house teams the difference they make to customers on the frontline?
- Are back of house staff members able to assist in basic ways if they are approached by a customer?

Creating a 'challenging' environment

Part of the tradition of service internally to an organisation is how open your leaders are to make things better for the end customers. Reflecting on and evolving the ways of working while being connected to changing customer needs is the way to future proof your organisation.

In Chapter 12, we explored the need to create a customer service meeting at the leadership level. This part of the chapter relates to that meeting and every other meeting you have as a leadership team. Between leaders of the organisation, there should be an environment where colleagues can 'challenge' each other for the best interests of the end customer. Having a leadership team who works together under a common goal with diverse opinions and points of view is the perfect recipe to creating a 'challenging' environment. This is not always the case.

While there may be good working relationships on the outside, some staff may be fearful of speaking up. They worry about getting other people off-side or worry that if they suggest something the other person will retaliate. Some leaders don't like to bring down others but like to be there when things don't work out so they can say 'I told you so'. All these concerns create a roadblock to the creative and innovative environment you need.

Let's look at a hypothetical scenario. An executive team is meeting to discuss the goals and plans for the week ahead. During the roundtable department update, the marketing manager outlines a campaign they are working on to boost customer engagement at an outdoor community event at the weekend. This manager feels that while they can make a creative event work well, it would help if they had someone from the operational department with them on the day to help provide information if a prospective customer asks a question.

The operations manager is extremely busy, concerned about staff overtime and doesn't like staff working on the weekends. The marketing manager wants to ask for some frontline support but is too afraid to suggest it because it may appear that they are shifting responsibility for a marketing campaign to an operational department. As a result, the community engagement session runs, but several customers who have questions on the day are told to phone the reception on Monday. The marketing manager regrets not asking for support but didn't have the courage to do so. The loser in all of this is the end customer.

Situations like this could be happening all the time in your organisation. We've spent a lot of time in this book discussing empowerment and permission, and sometimes leaders don't feel they have the permission to ask for help or delegate a task to another department that delivers a better outcome for the customer. This is not about making managers get involved in other portfolios just to be difficult. It's about everyone being included in discussions, and if someone has an idea that may work better – even if it requires more work by another party – they should not be afraid to speak up. Ideas within the business should be considered on their merit and impact on the customer, not based on who suggested it and their position.

In Chapter 12, we talked about frontline staff making suggestions on how to improve customer service and the overall experience. If this is something that is expected of frontline staff, then it should be expected from leaders too. Having your common purpose statement in the front of your mind at all meetings ensures that discussions are always focused on customers. You can imagine the leaders at Disneyland continuously being challenged on whether their ideas add to or detract from creating happiness.

An unknown author once wrote, 'A disagreement with someone turns into an argument, but a disagreement with a partner turns into a conversation.' When it comes to customer service, being aligned as a team is one thing, but it doesn't mean everyone needs to agree. Sometimes the most robust discussions that take time can lead to the best outcome for a customer that otherwise wouldn't have occurred.

If things turn into an argument, people should be able to walk away and return when they are ready for a healthy discussion. Heated discussions are not always a sign of conflict; they could be a sign of passion too. Different voices speaking up in meetings should be a good sign rather than hearing the same people agree for the sake of agreeing.

QUESTIONS TO CONSIDER

- Are your leaders comfortable in challenging others, including leaders, to do things differently to favourably impact customers?
- Do you feel people are afraid to speak up when it comes to improving customer service?
- Is your purpose statement used to guide discussions at leadership meetings?

Build a legacy based on non-negotiable service ethos

This is a book on culture, and while Chapter 5 explored some of the ways we define culture, I saved the word 'tradition' until this last chapter. Culture is all about tradition. If you think about cultures around the world, traditions are customs which have been passed on from generation to generation.

An organisational culture is the same as a tribal culture. Unless it's a family business, people aren't born into organisations, so they have a choice to come, stay or go. The traditions and culture of a business should be on the top of the list when someone is making an employment decision.

When looking at the culture and traditions of an organisation, people don't see how it fits around their employment–only 'in' their employment. For example, if you join an established company, the culture and traditions started before you joined and will continue well after you leave.

I mentioned in Chapter 11 that the Disneyland induction program is called 'Traditions'. This is a great example of how the tone is set for everyone who joins the business. The Walt Disney Company is one of the few worldwide that continues to trade based on the legacy of their founder. Many companies have continued to trade after their founder's death, but the Disney organisation makes a point of connecting to its origins.

While the organisation has evolved to keep with the times, many of the core values it was built on are relevant today. There's so much talk in business about change, and while change is important, it doesn't mean the core traditions need to be lost. For instance, I love eating pasta, and I love trying pasta whenever I go to a new restaurant, but I prefer it the way my mum cooks it, which is the same way her mum cooked it. My baba's (grandmother's) traditional pasta recipe lives on.

Not all organisations are built on the traditions such as Disney. Your organisation may be excelling at service, and you want to aim higher, or you may be early on in your service culture journey. There are many organisations who have only now made the decision to start making service part of their tradition when it previously hasn't been made a priority. A legacy of service is the final way to make your organisation renowned for service. We are simply not going to be around forever. Some of us will work in an organisation for a long time, others for a short time. Whichever way you look at it, as a leader you will eventually leave the organisation and unless it closes, someone else will take over your role.

During employment, leaders rarely think of a legacy in terms of what they will leave behind when they are no longer around. I once heard, 'Your legacy will be read later but is being written now.' Leaders need to think about what legacy they will leave behind while they are working.

When someone leaves an organisation, people will reflect on what that person meant to them and the business. They usually remember the humorous or quirky sides of a person: 'I always remember Bill. I love how he would talk about how he disagreed with the weekend's football umpiring every Monday morning.' Remembering someone's quirks is not leaving a legacy – it's simply leaving a memory. As the Walt Disney Company said, 'The best leadership legacy is not one that is fondly remembered, but one that is actively emulated.'[116] The legacy should be emulated well after someone leaves an organisation.

Using Bill as an example again, a legacy would be when someone says, 'I always remember Bill. At times he could be challenging to work with, but he never dropped his relentless passion to greet customers when they entered the office.' Traditions around service are built entirely on legacies like this.

The CEO can leave a profound legacy, but so can department managers and people on the frontline. Think of a legacy as the ripple of a stone thrown into a pond. If one stone is thrown in, there would be one set of ripples. This is what a CEO's legacy would look like, but if many stones were thrown in representing each leader, think about the number of ripples there will be. If all leaders view service in an aligned way, these ripples (or legacies) will make a profound difference to the organisation.

Creating a legacy starts by being a role model for others to follow. Following this book is a way to start. It's a lot to remember at first, but the more you work at it, you will begin to build a culture based entirely on service. If you can be relentless at it and agree it must be your focus for the entire time you work in an organisation, you are writing now what will be your legacy later.

A leader with a legacy of empowerment, who is relentless about service with a non-negotiable ethos will build the foundations for a thriving and lifelong service culture. We need to remind ourselves to think about the future when we are of service in the present.

Chinese philosopher Lao Tzu is claimed to have once said, 'When the best leader's work is done, the people say, "we did it ourselves".' While there is a lot of work involved for you as the leader, empowering the entire organisation to play their part in the culture will lead to this success.

As I conclude this final part of the book you can see that each chapter links into one another. For example, selection is the groundwork for education. Education is the groundwork for conversation. Conversation is the groundwork for recognition. Recognition is the groundwork for evaluation. Evaluation and tradition is what holds it all together.

QUESTIONS TO CONSIDER

- What service legacy are you writing now in your organisation?
- Would you change it?
- Is it something that people will just remember, or will they emulate it?
- Are you exemplifying what it means to be of service to be a role model for everyone else who follows you?

Conclusion

Thank you for taking the time to read this book. If this was your first read through, it now becomes a reference book for you to go back to and reflect on the strategies you didn't pick up on the first time.

Together we have embarked on a comprehensive exploration of cultures of service and the layering of the content and associated models has been designed for you to make logical sense of a big topic.

As service is different for everyone, the DNA of an organisational culture is just as unique. I believe in the value of an idea, and I am certain that after reading this book you will come up with new ideas to try within your organisation – I encourage you to give them a go.

The evolution of the three parts in this book has been designed with deliberate goals in mind. By the time you finished reading Part One: Excite, you should have been excited by the prospect of a culture of service. This means you not only understood what it was about, but also found yourself moving on the journey without thinking of excuses or flaws in the process.

After reading Part Two: Encourage, you should have started to see the picture of success more clearly, especially the everyday things in life that can be applied to service in the workplace. This should have become easier to implement at the more practical level. As you worked through the chapters, you may have been saying to yourself, 'Yes, this is something I can see forming in my organisation.'

Part Three: Exemplify was a practical look at how you can truly do just that – exemplify a service culture to everyone else in your organisation. While it was practical in the sense of the touchpoints with which you need to influence with your people, it should have challenged you to reflect on the other people within your leadership team and how you could get them to join you on this journey to support a cultural change. The employee touchpoints are commonly known to us all, and I hope that putting them together will help bring them into alignment with the core elements of a service culture from Part Two. Your employees will experience all these touchpoints in a seamless and elegant way. The reflective questions in each of the sections should help you take the first steps in how to move from reading to doing to being.

The way we serve one another changes over a variety of situations. Sometimes your teams will have the time to focus on service; other times, they may feel 'up against it'. The key theme of this book is how you empower everyone in your organisation to be of service when it's required. This includes during those busy and challenging times, or even during conflict situations where moralising is no longer the default response.

We've discussed that empowerment is not just about giving permission, and by being a leader who takes your organisation through the key stages of this book – exciting them, encouraging them and being an example for them – they will in turn be inspired to be of service to others. Your role as a leader is to lead, and this book gives you everything you need to do this from a service perspective. As you concentrate more on the service within your organisation and the relationship with others in the business, you will be best positioned to use your leadership qualities in the realms of service.

Don't forget our ambitious goals for what this book will help you achieve. Success might come quickly or slowly, but there is no reason you cannot climb the ladder and be renowned for your customer service and exceptional service culture. Reflect on the Introduction and think about the common issues we discussed embarking on this journey. By now you should be prepared to overcome these as you are equipped with the strategies you need.

If there's one thing that has been repeated throughout the book, it has been that service is all about how you are 'being' and not just what you're 'doing'. By now you might feel completely different about service compared to when you first started reading it. I encourage you to influence positively as many people as possible who will continue to spread this way of 'being' in life in general.

This book helps bring the best qualities out of you and your team and apply them to your work. As a result, I hope you feel more fulfilled in your role and the difference you are making to the lives of your colleagues and customers.

While this is not a self-help book, I find that, for me, the core principles are useful and practical when it comes to the difficult moments in life. Sometimes we need to see that a difficult moment in life can make us not respond at our best. If you lead a life where service to others is a theme, you will be the best person you can be as you respond to the challenges that come your way.

Earlier in the book I referred to Jeff Bezos's 1997 letter to the shareholders of Amazon. I want to close this book by citing something he said in that letter, something which is just as applicable today. He said:

'The one thing I love about customers is that they are divinely discontent. It's human nature. We didn't ascend from our hunter-gatherer days by being satisfied. People have a voracious appetite for a better way. I see that cycle of improvement happening at a faster rate than ever before.'[117]

If we think of our customers as being divinely discontent and having a voracious appetite for a better way, it will push us to strive to make our organisations renowned for the service we provide our customers well into the future.

When we look back to the top of the ladder of an exceptional service culture, we explored that it wasn't a journey to exceptional service, but about being exceptional on that journey. In reaching the top, I'm inspired to share a quote from Will Durant that is relevant more than ever after reading this book: 'We are what we repeatedly do; excellence, then, is not an act, but a habit.'

We discussed our intention in the book by introducing what it means to deliberately serve another person, which is always a wise choice. It requires discretion, and people should be free to serve, not feel forced. Customers may develop a positive memory in the moment, but the moment doesn't happen by chance. It's because we see the moment, and through brilliant execution, make it look like chance.

Many obstacles get in the way including shortcuts or the wrong advice. We must be wise in the path we choose to follow and be happy to reject anything that will drag the culture down and move us away from our goals.

I've written this book in complete service and shared as much as I possibly can in the format of a business book. Having said that, I understand the limitations of a written text and how some people may find this sufficient while others may need more help, which is why my business exists.

Notes

1 D Powell, '"Customers will just walk out": Coles exec flags "checkout-free" shopping within 10 years' (*The Sydney Morning Herald*, 13 January 2020), www.smh.com.au/business/companies/customers-will-just-walk-out-coles-exec-flags-checkout-free-stores-within-10-years-20200110-p53qbd.html, accessed December 2022
2 Dimension Data, www.dimensiondata.com/en-gb/insights/2020-global-cx-benchmarking-report, accessed December 2022
3 Disney Institute, 'Why Disney doesn't micromanage, it overmanages' (Inc., 24 January 2014), www.inc.com/disneyinstitute/james/overmanaging.html, accessed December 2022
4 SuperOffice, 'How a customer experience strategy helps scale revenue growth (and achieve profitability' (7 December 2022), www.superoffice.com/blog/customer-experience-strategy, accessed December 2022
5 J Bezos, '1997 letter to shareholders', www.sec.gov/Archives/edgar/data/1018724/000119312513151836/d511111dex991.htm, accessed January 2023
6 J Clear, '3-2-1: The responsibility of any creator, leadership, and how to succeed' (12 January 2023), https://jamesclear.com/3-2-1/january-12-2023, accessed January 2023

7   A Grant (@AdamMGrant) 'It takes curiosity to learn. . .'
    (13 September 2021), https://twitter.com/adammgrant/status/
    1437408114899357699?lang=en, accessed December 2022

8   J Hennessy, 'Embracing the need to "learn and relearn"' (*Stanford
    Magazine*, January/February 2002), https://stanfordmag.org/contents/
    embracing-the-need-to-learn-and-relearn, accessed December 2022

9   S Sinek (@simonsinek) 'Our best competitors. . .'(20 March 2018),
    https://twitter.com/simonsinek/status/976106508969824258?lang=
    en, accessed December 2022

10 G Tognini, 'Won't split the bill? Then we won't pay' (*The West
    Australian*, 30 January 2018), https://thewest.com.au/opinion/
    gemma-tognini/gemma-tognini-wont-split-the-bill-then-we-wont-
    pay-ng-b88728831z, accessed December 2022

11 'Bill Burlow on chain stores' (2018), www.youtube.com/
    watch?v=lOEID7wGk1k, accessed January 2023

12 Le Trèfle, 'Emma', www.adforum.com/creative-work/ad/
    player/34483612/emma/le-trefle, accessed January 2023

13 Rema 1000, 'Smart house', www.adforum.com/creative-work/ad/
    player/34579141/smart-house/rema-1000, accessed January 2023

14 J Hall, 'Woolworths investing $10million on training and
    store restructures' (News.com.au, 6 June 2019), www.news.
    com.au/finance/business/retail/woolworths-investing-
    10-million-on-training-and-store-restructures/news-story/
    b140f1b4b1c7bfd4c1d6c9becd8a7f5c, accessed December 2022

15 Telecommunications Industry Ombudsman, *Quarterly Report:
    Quarter 1 financial year 2022-23* (Telecommunications Industry
    Ombudsman), tio.com.au/sites/default/files/2022-11/TIO%202022-
    2023%20Q1%20Report_fa_LowRes.pdf, accessed 31 January 2023

16 K Vitasek, 'Building relationships: How to focus on individuals
    while dealing with many' (*Forbes*, nd), www.forbes.com/sites/
    katevitasek/2022/04/12/building-relationships-how-to-focus-on-
    individuals--while-dealing-with-many/?sh=43b3c39a652f, accessed
    December 2022

17 M Manson, *The Subtle Art of Not Giving a F*ck: A counterintuitive
    approach to living a good life* (Harper, 2016)

18 The Joy of Museums, 'Complaint tablet to Ea-Nasir – World's
    oldest complaint letter' (The Joy of Museums, 2022), https://
    joyofmuseums.com/museums/united-kingdom-museums/london-
    museums/british-museum/complaint-tablet-to-ea-nasir, accessed
    16 December 2022

19 E Visser, '33 years on: SA's servo sweethearts call it quits, put
    Klemzig's OG Speed Shop on market' (*The Advertiser*, 30 March
    2017), www.adelaidenow.com.au/messenger/north-northeast/33-
    years-on-sas-servo-sweethearts-call-it-quits-put-klemzigs-og-speed-
    shop-on-market/news-story/5bd3893adba4134b3f6d21dcaa91c0af,
    accessed December 2022

20 'Sam Neill talks acting' (2020), www.youtube.com/watch?v=-ScAktnImPbQ, accessed January 2023

21 T Alessandra, 'The Platinum Rule', www.alessandra.com/abouttony/aboutpr.asp, accessed 16 December 2022

22 M Manson (@IAmMarkManson) 'Commitment gives you freedom. . .' (9 April 2021), https://twitter.com/iammarkmanson/status/1380462244887199745?lang=en, accessed January 2023

23 M Manson, *The Subtle Art of Not Giving a F*ck: A counterintuitive approach to living a good life* (Harper, 2016)

24 C G Jung, *Memories, Dreams, Reflections* (Random House, 1973)

25 R Feloni, 'A Zappos employee had the company's longest customer-service call at 10 hours, 43 minutes' (*Business Insider*, 26 July 2016), www.businessinsider.com/zappos-employee-sets-record-for-longest-customer-service-call-2016-7, accessed December 2022

26 J Meyer (@jericho2785) 'Patience is not just waiting. . .', www.youtube.com/shorts/syjQ6ucfspk, accessed January 2023

27 J F Kennedy, 'We choose to go to the moon speech' (1962), www.youtube.com/watch?v=G6z-h6faR6o, accessed 16 December 2022

28 Insider Business, 'JFK's moonshot speech is still one of the most inspiring speeches ever delivered by a president' (2016), www.youtube.com/watch?v=G6z-h6faR6o, accessed December 2022

29 P Marsden, A Samson and N Upton, 'Advocacy drives growth: Customer advocacy drives UK business growth' (London School of Economics, December 2005), https://digitalwellbeing.org/wp-content/uploads/2015/05/Marsden-2005-06-Advocacy-Drives-Growth-Brand-Strategy.pdf, accessed December 2022

30 N Kano, 'What is the Kano Model' (Kanomodel.com, 2016), https://kanomodel.com, accessed January 2023

31 K Cotter, 'Answering your customer calls in our own backyard' (Telstra, 2021), https://exchange.telstra.com.au/answering-your-customer-support-calls-in-our-own-backyard, accessed 16 December 2022

32 T Puthiyamadam and J Reyes, 'Experience is everything: Here's how to get it right' (PwC, 2018), www.pwc.com/us/en/advisory-services/publications/consumer-intelligence-series/pwc-consumer-intelligence-series-customer-experience.pdf, accessed 16 December 2022

33 Buzztime Business, 'The Binge: Jon Taffer's expert advice for driving repeat business' (Buzztime, 6 September 2019), www.buzztime.com/business/blog/the-binge-jon-taffers-expert-advice-for-driving-repeat-business, accessed December 2022

34 J Collins, *Good to Great* (Random House Business, 2001)

35 D Powell, '"We like to stick to our knitting": Aldi rules out collectibles, loyalty programs' (*Sydney Morning Herald*, 29 July 2019), www.smh.com.au/business/companies/we-like-to-stick-to-our-knitting-aldi-rules-out-collectibles-loyalty-programs-20190729-p52bu5.html, accessed December 2022

36 MAJ Menezes and JD Serbin, 'Xerox Corp.: The customer
satisfaction program' (Harvard Business Publishing, 10 January
1991), https://hbsp.harvard.edu/product/591055-PDF-ENG,
accessed January 2023

37 S Ridley, *One Small Step. . . for Leaders: Practical actions to make you
a better leader today than you were yesterday* (Australian Institute of
Management, 2016)

38 N Merchant, 'Culture trumps strategy every time' (*Harvard Business
Review*, 22 March 2011), https://hbr.org/2011/03/culture-trumps-
strategy-every, accessed December 2022

39 Encyclopaedia Britannica, 'Mariana Trench', www.britannica.com/
place/Mariana-Trench, accessed December 2022

40 T Winter, 'Hire for attitude, train for skills. Sounds good, but'
(Human Performance Technology, 2012), https://blog.dtssydney.
com/hire-for-attitude-train-for-skills.-sounds-good-but, accessed 16
December 2022

41 Her Majesty Queen Elizabeth II, 'A speech by the Queen on her 21st
birthday, 1947' (21 April 1947), www.royal.uk/21st-birthday-speech-
21-april-1947, accessed December 2022

42 A Grant (@AdamMGrant) 'Personality is how you respond. . .'
(14 August 2021), https://twitter.com/adammgrant/status/
1426590475994034178?lang=en, accessed December 2022

43 HA Keller, *Helen Keller's Journal: 1936–1937* (Doubleday, Doran &
Company Inc, 1938)

44 Jim Roan, Facebook post (11 September 2017), www.facebook.com/
OfficialJimRohn/posts/only-by-giving-are-you-able-to-receive-
more-than-you-already-have-jim-rohn/10159284705245635, accessed
16 December 2022

45 A Grant (@AdamMGrant) 'Generosity is not a quest for
appreciation' (26 November 2022), https://twitter.com/
adammgrant/status/1596521921461780480, accessed January 2023

46 *Bluey*, Season 1 Episode 5: Shadowlands, www.bluey.tv/watch/
season-1/shadowlands, accessed January 2023

47 ACCAN, Telco Bushfire Response (8 January 2020), https://accan.
org.au/media-centre/hot-issues-blog/1684-telco-bushfire-response,
accessed 16 December 2022

48 B Fowler, 'Furious McDonald's customer calls cops after missing
breakfast cut off' (*NZ Herald*, 16 December 2021), www.nzherald.
co.nz/lifestyle/furious-mcdonalds-customer-calls-cops-after-
missing-breakfast-cut-off/LRJYEI62HS6KQOTNYMEQFWHRE4,
accessed December 2022

49 Ziffer, D, 'Banks still charging dead people months after, Royal
Commission Banking Code Compliance Committee finds' (ABC
News, 2020), www.abc.net.au/news/2020-08-31/banks-still-
charging-the-dead-bccc-finds-royal-commission/12614758, accessed
31 January 2023

50 J Laidler, 'NAB boosts customer help with 1000 extra sets of hands' (NAB News, 20 October 2021), https://news.nab.com.au/news/nab-boosts-customer-help-with-1000-extra-sets-of-hands, accessed December 2022

51 C Schelle, 'Stillwater at Crittenden winery charges $72 to cut birthday cake' (*Herald Sun*, 5 March 2018), www.heraldsun.com.au/news/victoria/stillwater-at-crittenden-winery-charges-72-to-cut-birthday-cake/news-story/bcee5df01ee1f4b23ce4282cc32b397d, accessed December 2022

52 DR Carney, AJC Cuddy and AJ Yap, 'Power posing: Brief nonverbal displays affect neuroendocrine levels and risk tolerance', *Psychological Science*, 21/10 (2010), 1363–1368, https://doi.org/10.1177/0956797610383437

53 J Peat, 'Thomas Cook staff go to work to try help passengers – despite losing their jobs' (*The London Economic*, 23 September 2019), www.thelondoneconomic.com/lifestyle/thomas-cook-staff-go-to-work-to-try-help-passengers-despite-losing-their-jobs-161379, accessed December 2022

54 R Blumenfeld, 'How a 15,000-year-old bone could help you through the coronacrisis' (*Forbes*, 21 March 2020), www.forbes.com/sites/remyblumenfeld/2020/03/21/how-a-15000-year-old-human-bone-could-help-you-through-the--coronavirus/?sh=2510628237e9, accessed December 2022

55 G Vaynerchuk, 'Road to twelve and a half: Kindness' (Garyvaynerchuk.com, 2 November 2021), https://garyvaynerchuk.com/road-to-twelve-and-a-half-kindness, accessed December 2022

56 N Larnaud, 'British movie theaters offer free tickets to "vulnerable" redheads during unprecedented heat wave' (CBS News, 22 July 2022), www.cbsnews.com/news/united-kingdom-movie-theaters-offer-free-tickets-redheads-amid-heat-wave, accessed December 2022

57 B Burr 'Customer care' (2019), www.youtube.com/watch?v=-89JN5GdMqb8, accessed January 2023

58 www.oxfordreference.com/display/10.1093/acref/9780191826719.001.0001/q-oro-ed4-00005454;jsessionid=BAC058FEE36F257857B4E68CFA9E3E76, accessed January 2023

59 A Grant (@AdamMGrant) 'When people go out of their way. . .' (28 September 2021), https://twitter.com/adammgrant/status/1442836440472330241?lang=en, accessed December 2022

60 F Reichheld, 'Prescription for cutting costs' (Bain & Company, nd), https://media.bain.com/Images/BB_Prescription_cutting_costs.pdf, accessed December 2022

61 Walker, 'How are customer satisfaction & retention linked & how do you improve them?', (The CX Leader Blog, 15 December 2021), https://walkerinfo.com/how-are-customer-satisfaction-and-retention-linked, accessed January 2023

62 Jumeriah, 'Jumeirah International rebrands' (21 June 2005), www.
    hospitalitynet.org/news/4023669.html, accessed January 2023
63 J Michelli, *The New Gold Standard: 5 leadership principles for creating
    a legendary customer experience courtesy of The Ritz-Carlton Hotel
    Company* (McGraw-Hill Education, 2008)
64 M Ludlow, 'CEOs are often blind to cultural problems' (*Financial
    Review*, 18 September 2019), www.afr.com/companies/professional-
    services/ceos-are-often-blind-to-cultural-problems-20190918-p52sjb,
    accessed December 2022
65 S Borys, 'Centrelink customers promised reduced wait times as
    Government hires 1,000 extra call centre operators' (ABC News,
    22 April 2018), www.abc.net.au/news/2018-04-23/government-
    promises-shorter-waiting-times-for-centrelink-custom/9685856,
    accessed December 2022
66 R Branson (@richardbranson) 'I've never had a desk. . .' (1 February
    2016), https://twitter.com/richardbranson/status/694234229950038
    017?lang=en, accessed December 2022
67 Coca-Cola, 'Happiness starts with a smile' (2015), https://
    adsofbrands.net/en/ads/coca-cola-happiness-starts-with-a-
    smile/9925, accessed January 2023
68 K Taylor, 'Chick-fil-A is beating every competitor by training
    workers to say "please" and "thank you"' (*Business Insider*,
    3 October 2016), www.businessinsider.com/chick-fil-a-is-the-most-
    polite-chain-2016-10, accessed December 2022
69 S Sinek (@simonsinek) 'Skills like effective. . .' (15 July 2021),
    https://twitter.com/simonsinek/status/1415768351520038919?ref_
    src=twsrc%5Etfw, accessed January 2023
70 S Sinek, *Start With Why* (Penguin, 2011)
71 The Disney Institute, 'Creating happiness: Small acts, big impact'
    (Disney Institute Blog, 28 July 2016), www.disneyinstitute.com/
    blog/creating-happiness-small-acts-big-impact, accessed December
    2022
72 The Disney Institute, 'Mission versus purpose: What's the
    difference?' (Disney Institute Blog, 23 October 2018), www.
    disneyinstitute.com/blog/mission-versus-purpose-whats-the-
    difference, accessed December 2022
73 T Puthiyamadam and J Reyes, 'Experience is everything: Here's how
    to get it right' (PricewaterhouseCoopers, nd), www.pwc.com/us/
    en/advisory-services/publications/consumer-intelligence-series/
    pwc-consumer-intelligence-series-customer-experience.pdf, accessed
    December 2022
74 Google, 'Google Cardboard Plastic', www.google.com/get/
    cardboard/plastic, accessed December 2022

75 Dutch News, 'Jumbo opens "chat checkouts" to combat loneliness among the elderly' (DutchNews, 28 September 2021), www.dutchnews.nl/news/2021/09/jumbo-opens-chat-checkouts-to-combat-loneliness-among-the-elderly, accessed December 2022

76 M Viejo, 'Carlos, the Spanish retiree taking on the banks' (*El Pais*, 20 January 2022), https://english.elpais.com/opinion/2022-01-20/carlos-the-spanish-retiree-taking-on-the-banks.html, accessed January 2023

77 J Hinchliffe, 'Queensland's happiest trolley collector pays it forward to thank Australia' (ABC News, 28 May 2019), www.abc.net.au/news/2019-05-28/happiest-trolley-collector-pays-it-forward-to-thank-australia/11152436, accessed December 2022

78 S Brown, *How to Talk So People Will Listen* (Baker Publishing Group, 2014)

79 B Harling, *How to Listen So People Will Talk* (Koorong, 2017)

80 BBC News, 'Apology after Japanese train departs 20 seconds early' (BBC News, 16 November 2017), www.bbc.com/news/world-asia-42009839, accessed December 2022

81 A Grant (@AdamMGrant) 'Acts of kindness shouldn't be. . .' (27 April 2022) https://twitter.com/adammgrant/status/1519332921408163842, accessed December 2022

82 CBC News, 'WestJet "Christmas miracle" video warms hearts on social media' (CBC News, 9 December 2013), www.cbc.ca/news/canada/calgary/westjet-christmas-miracle-video-warms-hearts-on-social-media-1.2457338, accessed December 2022

83 M Solomon, 'How the nation's most-awarded restaurant handles extreme customer expectations' (*Forbes*, 28 February 2015), www.forbes.com/sites/micahsolomon/2015/02/28/meeting-extreme-customer-expectations-a-lesson-from-the-nations-most-awarded-restaurant/?sh=2b06ad9f12ae, accessed December 2022

84 Booking.com, 'Booking right', www.adforum.com/creative-work/ad/player/34482776/booking-right/bookingcom, accessed January 2023

85 www.forbes.com/quotes/2024, accessed 16 December 2022

86 P Coelho (@paulocoelho) 'The world is changed by. . .' (2 June 2012), https://twitter.com/paulocoelho/status/209008454948495360?lang=en, accessed December 2022

87 V Gandhi and J Robison, 'The "great resignation" is really the "great discontent"' (Gallup, 22 July 2021), www.gallup.com/workplace/351545/great-resignation-really-great-discontent.aspx, accessed December 2022

88 A Soni, 'Talentica' (The Social People, 11 February, 2013), www.thesocialpeople.net/talentica, accessed December 2022

89 D Peppers, 'How Delta wins in customer service' (Inc., 14 April 2016), www.inc.com/linkedin/don-peppers/masterful -innovation-customer-feedback-don-peppers.html, accessed December 2022

90 Little Caesars Pizza Commercial (2008), www.youtube.com/ watch?v=HBdi0q6TXbw, accessed January 2023

91 A Apostolopoulos, 'Survey: 70% of employees in F&B businesses receive zero customer service training' (TalentLMS, 18 February 2019), www.talentlms.com/blog/employee-training-food-beverage-industry, accessed December 2022

92 A Watson, 'Disney Traditions: The first step to endless possibilities' (Disney Parks Blog, 14 October 2022), https://disneyparks.disney.go.com/blog/2022/10/disney-traditions-the-first-step-to-endless-possibilities, accessed December 2022

93 T Hsieh, *Delivering Happiness* (Hachette Book Group, 2010) p176

94 The Ritz-Carlton Leadership Center, 'Fostering great service' (The Ritz-Carlton Leadership Center, 19 March 2019), https:// ritzcarltonleadershipcenter.com/2019/03/19/fostering-great-service, accessed December 2022

95 4MAT 4learning, https://4mat4learning.com.au/what-is-4mat, accessed January 2023

96 von Goethe, JW, 'Maxim 281', in *Maxims and Reflections*, trans. Stopp (Penguin Classics, 1998)

97 MM Lombardo and RW Eichinger, *The Career Architect Development Planner*, 1st ed (Lominger, 1996)

98 R Carnahan, 'Tackle the first 90 days of your next role: A 5 step process for success on the job' (Harvard Business School Alumni, 21 April 2022), www.alumni.hbs.edu/careers/blog/post/tackle-the-first-90-days-of-your-next-role-a-5-step-process-for-success-on-the-job, accessed December 2022

99 GW Bush, 'Proclamation 6485 – National Customer Service Week', (The American Presidency Project, 8 October 1992), www.presidency.ucsb.edu/documents/proclamation-6485-national-customer-service-week-1992, accessed December 2022

100 J Childress, 'Will it make the boat go faster?' (Association For Talent Development, 9 September 2016), www.td.org/insights/will-it-make-the-boat-go-faster, accessed December 2022

101 J Bezos, '1997 letter to shareholders', www.sec.gov/Archives/ edgar/data/1018724/000119312513151836/d511111dex991.htm, accessed December 2022

102 A Oldenburg, 'Oprah's $7m car giveaway stuns TV audience' (USA Today, 14 July 2004), www.usatoday.com/story/life/2022/09/12/ oprahs-car-giveaway-tv-audience/10331572002/?gnt-cfr=1, accessed December 2022

103 S Godin, 'The simple truth about photo albums' (Seth's Blog, 7 September 2012), https://seths.blog/2012/09/a-simple-truth-about-photo-albums, accessed January 2023

104 B Wigert and A Mann, 'Give performance reviews that actually inspire employees' (Gallup, 25 September 2017), www.gallup.com/workplace/236135/give-performance-reviews-actually-inspire-employees.aspx, accessed January 2023

105 Digital Training Academy, 'Food case study: Honey Maid turns social media hate into love with diverse family campaign' (Digital Training Academy, nd), www.digitaltrainingacademy.com/casestudies/2014/09/honey_maid_turns_social_media_hate_into_love_with_diverse_family_campaign.php, accessed December 2022

106 Deloitte, 'Wealth management digitalization changes client advisory more than ever before' (Deloitte, 2016), www2.deloitte.com/content/dam/Deloitte/de/Documents/WM%20Digitalisierung.pdf, accessed December 2022

107 A Grant (@AdamMGrant) 'Seeking advice doesn't reveal incompetence...' (19 October 2021), https://twitter.com/adammgrant/status/1450475032312963075?lang=en, accessed December 2022

108 Statista, 'Social media marketing penetration in the U.S. 2013–2022' (Statistica Research Department, 2023), www.statista.com/statistics/203513/usage-trands-of-social-media-platforms-in-marketing/#statisticContainer, accessed January 2023

109 A Skores, 'Should you take your consumer gripe to the Better Business Bureau or Twitter?' (Techxplore, 22 June 2022), https://techxplore.com/news/2022-06-consumer-gripe-business-bureau-twitter.html, accessed December 2022

110 D Carroll, 'United breaks guitars', www.davecarrollmusic.com/songwriting/united-breaks-guitars, accessed December 2022

111 C Pochin, 'Restaurant has people in stitches over "worst ever" Tripadvisor review about coffee' (*Mirror*, 6 May 2022), www.mirror.co.uk/news/weird-news/restaurant-people-stitches-over-worst-26893487, accessed January 2023

112 T Nathalia, 'Garuda Indonesia bans photos on board its flights after bad review from vlogger' (Jakarta Globe, 16 July 2019), https://jakartaglobe.id/context/garuda-indonesia-bans-photos-on-board-its-flights-after-bad-review-from-vlogger, accessed December 2022

113 D Chau and S Letts, 'Meriton fined $3 million for interfering with negative TripAdvisor reviews' (ABC News, 31 July 2018), www.abc.net.au/news/2018-07-31/accc-trips-up-meriton-over-fake-reviews/10055618, accessed December 2022

114 ABC News, 'Online review promts "cease and desist" letter' (ABC News, 2017) www.abc.net.au/perth/programs/drive/online-reviews/9198746, accessed 1 February 2023

115 R Branson (@richardbranson) 'If you take care of your employees. . .'
     (15 August 2015), https://twitter.com/richardbranson/status/50027
     8499702480897?lang=en, accessed January 2023
116 The Disney Institute, 'A leadership legacy: Memories of Walt Disney'
     (The Disney Institute Blog, 5 February 2019), www.disneyinstitute.
     com/blog/a-leadership-legacy-memories-of-walt-disney, accessed
     December 2022
117   J Bezos, '1997 letter to shareholders', www.sec.gov/Archives/
     edgar/data/1018724/000119312513151836/d511111dex991.htm,
     accessed December 2022

Acknowledgements

Thank you to my beautiful wife, Breanna, for your ongoing support over the years from the first idea for the book, through to writing and publishing. The time spent on this book has taken me away from our young family for short periods of time, and I thank you for keeping things going while I dedicated myself to writing and editing. I hope this book will be a great legacy to leave for our sons Luka and Dominik, so they can read it when they are older and working in service to others.

To my mother-in-law and father-in-law, thank you for letting me use your home on the Collie River in the South West region of Western Australia while you were travelling. It was the perfect place to be inspired, uninterrupted and get the words out.

Andrew Horabin of the Bullshift Company, who I saw as a motivational speaker in school when I was twelve years old.

That unforgettable presentation stuck in my mind and was the motivation to do what I'm doing today. Thank you.

There are many friends and colleagues I have met through the speaking industry, many of whom have written books and given me advice, guidance and support early in my career. Thank you to David Koutsoukis, Margo Halbert, Rabia Siddique, Paula Smith, David Price, Thomas Murrell, Tasha Broomhall, Jenny Brockis, Todd Hutchison, Shirley Anne Fortina, Suzanne Waldron, Jeremy Watkins and Amanda Lambros. You make working in the industry and writing books feel less lonely as I know I have people to turn to.

Thank you to Lisa Evans and Andrea Gibbs who have both played a pivotal role in teaching me how to tell stories, which I have been able to bring to life throughout this book.

My accountability partner Kylie Denton for our monthly calls to ensure deadlines were met, progress is being made and just being on hand to work through things that needed a second ear.

There were four test readers who are also dear friends, and I would like to acknowledge each individually. Thank you for your generous time spent reading my manuscript in its early stages and providing me with the honest and constructive feedback to make the book what it is today.

Sarah Mitchell is the cofounder of Typeset, an editorial services company with offices in Australia, the UK and the US. She's on a mission to make the world a better place for readers everywhere.

Mike House is a speaker and mentor in adaptive thinking and a twenty-year veteran of survival instructing and organisational change. He is also the author of two books: *Thrive and Adapt: No matter what* and *(Un)shakeable: More than resilience.*

Andrea Walters is a communications leader with many years of experience at the helm of exemplary service delivery portfolios.

Wayne Crofts is an experienced CEO in customer- and market-led organisations.

To the team at Rethink Press: thank you to Lucy McCarraher, Joe Gregory and Casey Luxford for your generosity over your numerous webinars. To Bernadette Schewerdt for your words of wisdom and coaching through the writing phase, and to Julie Brown, Susan Furber, Abi Willford and Kerry Boettcher for editing my manuscript. Thanks also to Stefan Banovich for assisting me in reviewing the publishing contract.

Special thanks to my designer Tracey Skinner for taking my hand drawings and converting them into the fifteen amazing models throughout this book.

Finally, but most certainly not least, I would like to thank every one of my clients for entrusting me with your organisation. To those who have participated in my workshops, thank you for your feedback, questions and engagement, which has certainly helped me shape all my content in service to you.

The Author

Chris Smoje has always been fascinated by what it means to be of service to others. He has seen how this works directly on the frontline, in leadership roles and in the classroom. Chris is proud to have worked for global service brands such as Qantas, where he developed practical experience in the deployment of significant culture transformation projects and the overall difference this can make.

Learning is Chris's passion. He is an educator and holds postgraduate qualifications in Adult and Tertiary Education. Chris has also been most fortunate to have been formally trained by the Disney Institute. This has not only given Chris the exposure to one of the world's leading service organisations, but it has also enabled him to see first-hand the patterns and trends that exist in other world-class brands that make their service stand out.

Organisations that Chris has worked with have seen direct uplifts with their service and have been honoured with industry awards in customer service and training excellence in recognition of the unrelenting partnership, focus and commitment to customer service. Chris has also been a judge for numerous state and national awards in the service excellence category.

It is an exciting time for organisations, with endless opportunities and potential for organisations who take this step. The world is talking about service and culture and Chris is sought after to comment on service issues and trends in print, radio and television media, so he must remain aware of what's happening in the ever-changing customer service landscape.

Chris is a Certified Speaking Professional, which is an international designation placing him in the top echelon of speakers globally. Certified Speaking Professionals have a high level of experience in their business and the industry as well as a proven track record of capturing the audience and consistently delivering value from the stage. Chris is also a Fellow of the Australian Institute of Management in Western Australia.

⊕ www.chrissmoje.com

▣ www.linkedin.com/in/chrissmoje

🐦 @ChrisSmoje

Index

technical skill 161, 194
technology 5–6, 29–30, 33
telecommunications 31, 66–8, 74, 114
Telecommunications Industry
    Ombudsman 31
Telstra 75
theme/amusement park/leisure
    20, 145, 268–9, 280–2
thinking stairs 164
ThinkJar 31
Thomas Cook 121
to-do list 156
Toffler, Alvin 17
Touche 252
touchpoints 12, 91–2, 177, 190, 194,
    216, 277–8, 290
tradition 191, 271
    challenging environment,
        creating 282–5
    colleagues as internal customers
        271–3
    non-negotiable service ethos
        285–8
    relies on someone for service
        274–7
    supportive environment,
        creating 277–82
training 35, 96–7, 205
    classroom 40
    courses 40
    customer service 39–40, 206
    departments 9
    employees 30
    limitations in 220
    on-the-job service 215, 218
    programs 4, 36, 47
transformational programs 81

tribal culture 285
TripAdvisor 82, 261, 263
Twitter 34, 256
two-way communication 171, 201
Tzu, Lao 288

Uber (rideshare) 64, 253
umpires/referees 25, 96, 112
University of Texas 260
unlearning service 16, 16–17
Utopia 196

Vaynerchuk, Gary 124

Walker, Jason 196
Walt Disney Company 7, 165, 207,
    286–7; see also Disney, Walt;
    Disney Institute
Walt Disney World 198; see also
    Disneyland
wants and emotions versus needs
    and stereotypes 67
Weinstein, Steven 54–5
Westin Hotel, Bali 157
WestJet 175
winery 116
Winfrey, Oprah 241
Woolworths (supermarkets) 30, 81
working relationships model 9, 10
work-life balance 118
work-related conversation 224

Xerox 84

Yap, Andy 120

Zappos 54–5, 207, 280

Manufactured by Amazon.com.au
Sydney, New South Wales, Australia